SMART
DIVERSIFICATION
(IN REAL ESTATE)

SMART DIVERSIFICATION (IN REAL ESTATE)

The Ultimate Guide To Maximizing Your Money As An Intelligent Real Estate Investor

FUQUAN BILAL

Printed in the United States of America.
First paperback edition June 2022.

Cover design by Mocah Studio, LLC
Layout design by G Sharp Design, LLC.

ISBN 979-8-9864816-0-9 (paperback)

Contents

Preface

This book was created to help enhance understanding of how to apply diversification in real estate investing to get the best possible financial results throughout your lifetime, and even beyond.

At the time of writing, this is the first real book about this essential subject and a vital part of your money game. The lack of access to this information has bankrupted billionaires; that same access has minted multi-millionaires.

Sadly, 99% of the information being fed to us is just to sell us on a financial product that is great for the person selling it, but leaves out the most basic and key ingredients to both achieving and maintaining financial success.

This is the missing piece of the puzzle that you need.

For more than 20 years, I've tried diversifying into all types of businesses. I've tried just about every type of real estate investment strategy and asset class you've heard of, and probably a few more that you haven't.

There is no question that real estate is the greatest investment you can make. It is the application of how you do it that makes *all* the difference.

Just like you can buy the ingredients for a fantastic meal, but if you just slap it on a plate without following the cooking directions and leave something out, your stomach won't feel too good. You probably won't get the health benefits or blissful outcome you expected and craved, either.

As I have grown wiser through trials and errors, and have been blessed with strokes of luck, I've yearned to find and focused on finding a better solution. In the process, I discovered the key to winning at investing, optimizing for the best financial performance now, and future-proofing your money.

The result is a formula that gives you the best risk-based returns, lifestyle, and financial benefits in the now, without sacrificing your future finances. You can stay strong now, and be confident about meeting your financial goals throughout your life and achieving your bolder ideals for retiring and beyond.

Many of those I've helped are accredited investors, high-income-earning busy working professionals, family offices, and even fund managers, but this is crucial and fundamental knowledge for everyone. Whether you are 10 years old and believe there has to be a better way to do life and money; are in college; are a single parent, working three jobs for minimum wage and want to break out of the rat race; or want to run your own investment firm, this is for you.

Without this information, you will be seduced into a lot of detours and financial black holes. I don't want that for you. I've done the testing and trials, and put in the blood, sweat, tears, and years to get it right — along with my own money — so you don't have to. Take the path that's already been paved for you.

Contrary to just about everything else you'll ever read, I'm not going to tell you there is only one best way to invest or get involved in real estate. That's a con. However, I will show you how to take the best of every financial discipline and strategy that has been used by 90% of millionaires and all billionaires, all so that you can skip the pitfalls, and stay on the faster, safer, and far more profitable right track.

Whether you've been burned in trying to diversify by listening to brokers or trying DIY real estate investing, or you are already doing very well, this will complete the loop and connect the dots for you so you stop leaving so much on the table, don't make bankrupting mistakes, and continuously prosper instead.

This information is especially for those who want to get ahead financially; protect the wealth they are building; insulate themselves from pandemics and deep recessions; and make sure they are enjoying the maximum upside when it's raining real estate gold out there.

Introduction

If you've ever asked a traditional investment advisor or broker about what to do with your money, clicked through a few articles on a financial website, or even walked through the aisles of a bookstore like people used to do, you've probably heard about the concept of diversification.

It is a key investment principle. It is necessary. Yet it can be dangerous and counterproductive when not applied correctly. That's a big part of the reason for publishing this book.

Even those who have been lifelong raving fans of other types of investments and asset classes cannot deny that real estate is one of the best things to invest in, if not hands down *the* best.

Why? Because 90% of millionaires made their money from real estate. You can't name any billionaires who don't own a pretty good slice of it, either. Even those who may appear famous for something else now owe a lot of their income and wealth to real estate.

Of course, there are risks that apply to real estate. You've probably been bombarded with all types of strategies and tactics and real estate asset "opportunities." You may have even tried some of them for yourself, and you might have found out they are a lot harder, more complicated, and less guaranteed than expected.

Again, it is all about the execution, and how you do it. In this book, we'll take a look at different types of investment strategies and assets, with a fresh, realistic, and transparent perspective on their pros and cons, weaknesses, and strengths.

We'll dive into the number one mistake that virtually everyone makes — plus the cure for it.

You'll learn about how not to blow it all with a distorted view or misunderstanding of what diversification is about, and how to balance wise diversification intelligently, with all the advantages of focus.

You'll learn what's better, especially for how to meet your immediate, medium-term, and long-term goals.

And perhaps most importantly: how to get started for yourself.

Why do I give and share this info? No one has up to this point. Maybe I just think differently. I believe there is plenty of prosperity out there for everyone if they are willing to take action for themselves — and act on the right information. A rising tide lifts all boats. We can do a lot of good together if we are all more prosperous. Not many people in the banking and brokerage world seem to think like this yet, although that's why we need this information, isn't it?

Whether or not you've invested in real estate, feel like you've flopped at it in the past or recently, or run a sizable fund or company, you will find a fresh take and new perspective on investing that just might change everything.

Chapter 1

REAL ESTATE AS AN INVESTMENT CLASS

Real estate, income, and wealth have been inseparably connected since humans have been on Earth. In fact, as we go to Mars and further into space, this will also undoubtedly remain true everywhere, forever.

Real estate is an indivisible part of building and protecting wealth and generating income.

Don't believe it? Just take a look at the wealthiest people throughout history and how they've made their money, or at least kept it and multiplied it.

While history gets a little murky when you go back to 3,000 to 5,000 BC, even then, wealth is synonymous with control over land. That's when the first ancient Egyptian kings came along as they developed irrigation along the Nile River, unified lands, built new types of housing and architecture, and invented luxury. Of course, the pyramids are still a big draw and income producer from tourism today, 5,000 years later.

During the years of the Roman Republic, Marcus Crassus (who was born in 115 BC) grew his wealth by seizing property from people he had sent to jail and had executed, as well as buying up whole neighborhoods of distressed property. His net worth was estimated at around $20B.

Born in 63 BC, Caesar Augustus, of the Roman Empire, was worth an estimated $4.6T, according to *Time* magazine, thanks to personally owning all of Egypt.

Fast-forward to the Middle Ages, and you had the conquests of the Normans and English kings. During this time, Alan Rufus became a notable income property owner, worth an estimated $194B, according to Money.com.

In the 1800s in the U.S., you had the likes of Carnegie and Rockefeller, both of whom still have their names on property and were worth an estimated $350B each.

More recently, lists of the richest people alive include names like Jeff Bezos, Mark Zuckerberg, Warren Buffett, Larry Ellison, and Bill Gates. While some may be more famous for other things, they are among America's most significant real estate investors and landlords. Bezos has sold off a lot of Amazon stock to invest in his personal real estate portfolio. Zuckerberg has become rather infamous for his prime property investments. Ellison bought an island. Buffett still counts real estate as his best investment, after marrying his wife; his mortgage lending and real estate companies carried him through the 2018 financial crisis. Gates has become one of the largest property owners in the world and the largest owner of farmland in the U.S., with around 250,000 acres, worth around $700M — not including his homes and other real estate investments.

The bottom line seems to be that you might have made a name for yourself in a quick career sprint in a variety of things, but ultimately, if you want to preserve those gains, grow your income, and create lasting wealth, it's all about real estate.

THE FOUR PILLARS OF REAL ESTATE INVESTMENT

You are probably well aware of these benefits by now, but they cannot be overstated. Intelligent, wealthy investors don't get distracted by fad investments and money pitfalls, because they remember these four pillars that real estate offers.

1. Wealth Growth

Growing your wealth is essential. That's true whether you are starting out with $10k or $10B.

It's not possible to stay static. There is such a wide range of threats to your wealth and its value that you have to keep growing. If you aren't growing, you are sinking.

Just consider inflation and the devaluation of money. In the year before writing this book, real inflation at the store for many items was around 30%. That means if you had $1M in the bank 12 months ago, it would only buy you around $700k worth of things. If that keeps up for just one more year, your $1M would only buy you $490k worth of things. You can see that in just a few years, it won't be worth much at all.

According to some valuations, the value of a dollar changed by almost 1,500% between 1942 and 2021. Not for the better, either.

If your grandparents saved you $1 from back then, it used to be able to buy a lot more than it can today. In 1955, you could have bought two entire meals at McDonald's for just 70 cents. In 1963, a movie ticket cost just 86 cents; now just a bottle of water at the movie theater can cost you six times that much. In 1967, you could have bought three gallons of gas for less than a dollar; now one gallon of gas is well over $3.

You get the idea, right? *Just holding onto cash money is the fastest way to lose it.*

One of the big benefits of real estate is that it typically goes up in line with, or better than, inflation. That can apply to rents and cash flows, as well as the value of assets.

Consider the average home price in the United States. While there are certainly ups and downs, like in anything else, these make the money invested in your home worth more rather than less.

Consider that in the wake of COVID lockdowns, some grocery items and lumber prices may have gone up by 30%. Yet property prices and rents were frequently up from 30% to over 70%. Some even higher than that.

This is organic, passive wealth growth. It's a gift. You really don't have to do anything for it after you acquire the asset. Of course, there can be maintenance costs, repairs, etc., but the land value alone will appreciate and see equity growth.

In addition to this organic growth and equity windfall, many ways to grow this wealth through value-add methods exist.

You can build on it; expand improvements; make updates; market it better; optimize management and operations; increase rents; develop timber, mineral, oil, and air rights; and much more.

Challenges to your wealth growth can include:

- Inflation
- Investments that lose money
- Low yield investments
- Poor asset management
- Taxes

What helps you grow your wealth?

- Appreciation
- Inflation-beating returns
- Compounding returns
- Strong risk-adjusted returns

2. Wealth Protection

Making a million dollars isn't nearly as challenging as multiplying or retaining it. All types of threats to your wealth, net worth, and nest egg exist. Real estate-related investments offer enduring wealth. They are tangible. They can survive inflation, wildfires, hurricanes, and more — the land where the bulk of the value lies will still be there.

Maintaining that stronghold of wealth and capital provides other opportunities to multiply it and generate income with it. That's a whole lot better than becoming a one-minute millionaire in the next cryptocurrency or stock before it flashes, crashes, and evaporates.

Real estate inherently grows in value. Of course, price dips occur, but the market usually recovers. If you're in it for the long term, you'll most likely see significant gains, which implies more earnings when it comes time to sell. Real estate investments are popular long-term retirement plans for many people.

The physical tangibility of real estate provides great security. Yet it is also important to be sure you are not grossly overpaying at the top of the cycle and positioning yourself for an obvious dip or are not sinking money into losing assets.

3. Income Generation

Income is vital to all of us. You can have the biggest nest egg, and yet see it all burned away in just a few years if you are spending your savings instead of the income it produces.

This is why most lottery winners go bankrupt within a few years. It's why many multi-million-dollar athletes and Hollywood celebrities end up broke. It's why most big family inheritances are completely gone within a generation or two.

Real estate offers the ability not just to create income, but to create income from your capital, and make your money work for you, instead of always having to work for money.

It offers two vital features of its income potential: recurring and passive income. That means once you are invested in a property, it can go on delivering a lifetime of income. It can deliver multi-generational income into infinity. Even young mortgage notes can deliver 20 to

30 years of income. In many cases, those borrowers and their families also become lifetime sources of income. This is the most prized type of income for sophisticated investors, along with venture capital, private equity, and endowment and pension funds.

Passive income is income that keeps on coming in even if you aren't doing anything for it. It shows up if you've been sleeping all day, were stuck in the hospital for months, have been on an extended vacation, went to volunteer for a few weeks, have been too busy taking care of family members to work, or simply can't physically or mentally work anymore. It detaches your income-generation abilities from your capabilities and the number of hours you can work in a day. The sooner you begin benefiting from it, the more freedom you will have. This may sound basic for experienced investors, but even those who have been in this space for years often neglect having sufficient levels of passive income.

If you don't need the extra income yet, then you can reinvest it to compound the gains on your investments.

4. Tax Savings

The number one threat to income, wealth growth, and retaining wealth is often taxes, not one of those fly-by-night scams that pops up and disappears. Taxes take the biggest bite out of your efforts to grow and maintain wealth. Taxation just seems to consistently grow as a threat. At the time of writing, new layers of taxes were attempting to eat up as much as 60% of capital gains in some states. That doesn't even count the initial income taxes on that money, transfer taxes to acquire those things, and sales or inheritance and death taxes if you spend it or try to pass it on.

Tax Freedom Day, the day when analysts expect the average person in each state to have worked long enough each year to pay their federal, state, and local taxes, seems to come later and later. In places like Washington, D.C., and New York City, most people will work until June each year just to cover their annual taxes. It's quite likely that it will be much longer each year for many, once you calculate all the taxes you really pay. Did you realize you were literally working almost six months each year or more before you turned a penny in profit that you could keep? That's half of your life just on taxes.

Remember, it is not how much you make or win; it is how much you get to keep that really matters. You can win $1M in a lottery, and only receive $500k after taxes — or you can make $1M gain on the sale of a property, and if the transaction is structured well, pay no taxes. Which would you prefer?

Some of the ways you can reduce your taxes within real estate investing include the following:

Operating as a Real Estate Investment Business

This may provide an additional layer of tax breaks because you could be able to write off qualified business expenses, including a home office, transportation and travel, business services, dining and entertainment, and capital investments and temporary paper losses.

You can avoid the double taxation of a C corporation by organizing your entity as an LLC, partnership, or S corp.

Depreciation

Depreciation can provide substantial tax breaks, while also being one of the few tax breaks that you can actually add back to use to qualify for loans and other credit from lenders, without paying more taxes.

The premise is that some things depreciate or lose value over time as they age, such as appliances or roofs. Various types of property benefit from different depreciation schedules and time frames, such as residential versus commercial, and mobile homes versus new construction properties.

Capital Gains Taxes

When you sell an item, such as a piece of property, for a profit, you may be subject to capital gains tax. Short-term and long-term are the two categories to be mindful of. They each have a distinct influence on your tax rates.

A short-term capital gain occurs when you earn from selling an asset within a year of purchasing it. You may be forced to sell, but be aware that doing so may have a negative impact on your taxes. This is because the gain is considered ordinary income.

If you make $100,000 from your day job and sell an investment property for $100,000 profit, your taxable income effectively doubles. This can put you in a whole new tax bracket.

On the other hand, if you benefit from the sale of an asset that you've owned for a year or more, you'll experience a long-term capital gain. If you can hold off on selling until the anniversary of your purchase, you'll be able to keep extra money in your pocket. This is due to the fact that the long-term capital gains tax rate has often been much lower than the regular income tax rate.

1031 Exchanges

1031 exchanges reward people who reinvest their investment gains. This program allows you to exchange properties for tax purposes as long as the new property you acquire is similar in concept. That is, you can postpone paying the capital gains tax on the first property's sale.

1031 exchanges can be used forever. However, if you wish to cash out your gains, you must pay any taxes that are required. Depending on the date of your buy and sell transactions, a few versions of the application are accessible, including reverse exchanges. Because specific rules and timelines apply, it is recommended that you talk with a skilled financial practitioner before trying it.

Opportunity Zones

Opportunity Zones are among the special economic zones designated for redevelopment that can provide tax breaks to investors and businesses moving into an area.

Opportunity Zones are often low-income or disadvantaged areas of property as designated by the U.S. Department of the Treasury. By providing tax advantages, the 2017 Tax Cuts and Jobs Act encourages investors to spend money on expanding and economically stimulating these regions. You invest your unrealized capital gains in an Opportunity Zone alongside other investors. You defer taxes for years, or enjoy tax-free returns.

Retirement Accounts

You've undoubtedly heard of IRAs and Roth IRAs as tax-advantaged ways to save for retirement. What you might not realize is that you can create your own self-directed IRA and use it to invest in real estate tax-free, or with deferred taxes.

To begin, you must choose a custodian or trust business to manage your self-directed IRA. They set up the self-directed IRA, and you deposit funds into it. After that, you can form a legal entity, such as an LLC, to acquire and hold investment properties. The self-directed IRA invests funds in the legal entity of your choice.

When you wish to finance an investment property rather than pay cash for it, the loan must be nonrecourse, which means the borrower cannot be held personally accountable, which some lenders do not allow.

Learn how to take advantage of the tax benefits available to real estate investors. They can save you hundreds of thousands of dollars, allowing you to devote more of your money to growing wealth.

It's true that taxes, tax rates, and tax rules are changing all the time — but real estate can offer many different and multiple layers of tax protections. That makes it better for income, wealth protection and growth, and your legacy.

The bottom line here is that you can't reasonably expect to defend and maintain your current status, income, and wealth without real estate investments in your portfolio. You certainly can't hope to sustainably grow those resources without it, or truly get ahead. No matter what you aspire to in quality of life, control over your life, and opportunities for those you care about, this is a vital part of what you do with your money — perhaps the most important thing you can do. That applies whether you are working three jobs for minimum wage and don't have enough financial room to even breathe, or you are vying for top spot on the *Forbes* Richest List and have tens of billions in net worth. Chances are you don't have nearly enough of it yet.

Of course, lots of myths, misinformation, and misunderstandings about real estate-related investments persist. Let's bust through some of those so you can invest more safely and more profitably, and with confidence.

Chapter 2

THE PROS & CONS OF POPULAR REAL ESTATE INVESTMENTS: HOW TO OPTIMIZE THEM

You know you absolutely *must* invest in real estate. The big question many are wrestling with and debating is *how* to do it.

There are many ways to invest in the real estate sector. Creative spin-offs and hybrid options continue to emerge. Let's take a look at the most common and popular core investment strategies. These are the go-to strategies and foundations for everything else.

Specifically, let's look at the pros and cons of these methods — what they are best at delivering, as well as the risks that many try to avoid talking about, and how to intelligently optimize for lower risk, maximum upside, and the optimal risk adjusted returns.

If we don't do this, then it is like investing blindfolded, walking in the dark. You may either be too afraid of the unknown to make any progress, or you'll fall into a hole, and blame the blindfold, even though you could have just taken that blindfold off your own head.

HOUSE-FLIPPING

What it Is

You've probably seen it on TV or in ads online on YouTube or in your favorite social media apps.

House-flipping is the process of buying a property, giving it an inexpensive makeover, and reselling it for (often a lot) more than you paid for it.

This can be applied not just to homes but to any property type, from land to shopping malls, office buildings, industrial real estate, multi-family apartment buildings, and more.

This umbrella might also cover wholesaling real estate, and optimizing and adding value by enhancing performance and financials before reselling.

At its core, flipping is about acquiring undervalued or underperforming assets, unlocking and adding value, and then cashing in on those improvements for a profit.

This has become a trendy way to make money in recent years. Hollywood celebrities have jumped on it. Fashion moguls like Tommy Hilfiger have gotten into it. Rappers have done it. TV Realtors and flippers have become mini-celebrities vying for their 15 minutes of fame.

The Pros

The big draw to flipping is probably the size of the profits.

House-flipping has certainly delivered big lump-sum profits and high rates of returns.

According to ATTOM Data, the average gross profit per house flipped has often been around $60,000. That's more than some people make in a year, working full-time. Flipping two houses a year can generate more than even bankers at big financial firms like Goldman Sachs earn or software technicians at Google make. You don't even have to take out student loans and spend four years of your life at college to do it.

There are flippers who make 100% returns, or who make millions per unit by flipping luxury homes and estates. Some turn over hundreds of units each year.

Some like this as a way to flex their creativity and design ideas; although it is important to remember that an investment is best when it is most business-like, and to differentiate between investments and hobbies.

One of the most significant, yet often overlooked, pros of this strategy is improving and saving communities and neighborhoods. The impact you can have can be pretty amazing if you approach it as an opportunity to create good jobs; make communities safer, cleaner, and healthier; and create a legacy impact that can last for generations.

The Gotchas

There are a variety of pitfalls that house-flippers notoriously fall into.

Net profitability is one of them. TV shows about flipping have become incredibly dangerous. It wouldn't be surprising if some lawsuits occur over them in the future.

They like to throw vague numbers up on the screen and make it sound like they are making a lot of money. However, there can be substantial differences between the gross profits these actors claim and the real net profits on those deals. They rarely factor in all the costs or taxes on their profits. Many would be in the red once the full math was done.

Profitably flipping properties requires that you get your numbers right. The most obvious of these is how much you pay for a property. You need a significant cushion to be able to account for transactional costs, improvements and repairs, marketing, hold time, and taxes, as well as being able to offer an attractive deal to your end buyers and staying profitable in a constantly fluctuating market.

Rehabbing projects also always, always, *always* cost more than you plan, and take longer to complete than you think. You must build in enough of a financial cushion to your numbers not to take a loss.

This also rolls over into operating profitability and costs of building materials and labor. These figures can fluctuate significantly, too. Individual and small house-flipping operations are at great risk exposure and can't compete competitively with longer-established and higher-volume operators who are able to command the fastest service and best discounts on these things.

It only takes running out of money on one deal before the renovations are complete for a newer individual house-flipper to end up with a deadweight property that they can't afford to keep or sell. That one money pit can bankrupt you.

Other common issues are trying to DIY all the renovations, over-improving properties, and being too slow to turn a property and getting caught by a changing market.

This is an intensive business that can be hugely profitable but can bankrupt you fast if you are going it alone on a small scale with limited resources.

Pro Tips for the Modern Intelligent Investor

Sustainable success in flipping relies on factoring for risk-adjusted returns when pricing acquisition offers and refusing to overpay, no matter what others are doing in the market.

It's important to have a healthy appreciation for the power of volume and established industry relationships. This leads to profitable and smooth-flowing acquisition and disposition channels.

Perhaps most importantly: Contractors will make or break you, despite everything else. It doesn't matter how cheaply you got the deal or how hot the market is. Without strong relationships with great contractors you can trust, nothing will work out well.

RENTALS

What it Is

Rentals are a buy-and-hold or income property strategy. This can apply to virtually any property type, from raw land to industrial buildings. To keep this focused, we will home in on single-family and multi-family apartment rentals for this section.

Rentals can be short- or long-term and involve any type of property. The concept is essentially the same. It is all about acquiring an asset with income-producing potential. Those assets may already be producing income and underperforming their potential, or they may be nonperforming and ready for repositioning.

The Pros

Rentals are powerful — perhaps one of the most powerful investment strategies — because they bring everything together. All the essential advantages and benefits of real estate investing can come together in a rental property portfolio, if done well.

They offer the potential to grow wealth, either passively and organically, or through value-add strategies. They can generate income and cash every month. They provide a variety of tax-saving opportunities.

Along with very competitive yields, rentals offer something most other high-yielding investments don't: the security of a tangible asset and downside protection. Overall, they are highly recession-resistant.

And they offer all of this at the same time in one investment.

While income properties can be flipped, one of their great draws is low transaction costs, because you are not constantly buying and turning them like house-flips or stocks.

We are also talking about residual, long-term, and even multi-generational income and wealth.

The Gotchas

Despite all the crucial upsides for your finances and portfolio, rentals can also become a nightmare for those who underestimate the work involved and who fail to prepare for and understand the nuances of this asset class.

Unexpected costs are a common gotcha with rentals. These costs are often big and can eat up a lot of potential profit and income. For example, if you only have one rental unit, the AC blows out in the middle of summer, and you were only netting $500 per month, that $6,000 replacement could wipe out a year of income. If anything else comes up, you'd be in the red.

Of course, ways to minimize these risks and dramatically reduce the expense exist, but new and solo investors often don't know them.

Disasters and interruptions can be frequent in some geographic areas. If you have a rental house in Miami or New Orleans, it's not a matter of if, but how often, hurricanes are going to come through, and how hard they are going to hit the next time.

The same goes for wildfires in parts of California, or tornadoes in Kansas.

Then there are landlord-tenant laws and regulations. They are complex and can vary a lot between locations. Each state, county, and city may have their own overlays, some of the most notable being rent controls and eviction bans. This is a hyper-litigious environment in the U.S. One mistake or flawed interaction and you can be giving away your money, property, and other assets. The COVID era also introduced federal bans against evictions and even removed some of the landlord protections in charging rent during the pandemic.

You also need to know that DIY property management is far more intensive and expensive than you can ever imagine, at least until you get elbow- and neck-deep in it. The truth is that DIY property management means no freedom. As a solo or "mom and pop" landlord, you don't get any of those promised freedoms. There is nothing passive about it. You are on call 24/7, 365 days a year. There is no such thing as vacation time.

The dream of rentals that are sold by Facebook gurus and most infomercials may often be a scam. Yet, done well, they are critical to your finances and are inseparable from creating and maintaining real wealth for everyone.

Pro Tips for the Modern Intelligent Investor

The number one ingredient in the recipe for success in rentals is to always, *always* use professional property management from day one.

This will greatly enhance performance, while minimizing exposure to risk. Next to contractors, property management is one of the top two influential factors.

The best investment opportunity in the world can be destroyed in just a few days by poor property management, while great property management can make even a mediocre investment outperform.

The second key here is diversification. This is what will make all the difference in sustainability, continuity, consistent returns, and minimizing the impact of all those risks we've covered.

MORTGAGE LOAN NOTES

What it Is

Debt investing in the form of mortgage loan notes is another strong real estate strategy. I'm proud to say that I've been involved in pioneering what you might call the "democratization of mortgage note investing" since 2008.

Since then, there has been far greater access to investing in various types of mortgage debt and at many different levels.

The concept is simply taking a page out of the bank's playbook, but doing it much better on the servicing side.

You can buy big pools of mortgage loans, or sometimes individual mortgage loan notes. You become the "bank" or lender. As the noteholder, you have an asset that can produce ongoing monthly income as the borrower makes their payments. It's passive cash flow, with very strong yields.

These notes are acquired at some level of discount. Often they are traded based upon a percentage of the unpaid principal balance. Your investment is secured by the physical property as collateral.

These assets can be improved in value and flipped, or you can sell partial notes, retaining a portion of ongoing payments while receiving a lump sum of cash upfront.

The Pros

Mortgage note investing has many great advantages. It has been the big banks' go-to strategy for accumulating massive wealth and billions in revenue for years, so there has to be something good about it.

One of the main reasons I was drawn to it, at the suggestion of my son, was to help borrowers. Banks and lenders have done a notoriously horrific job of serving borrowers. We saw that in the 2008 foreclosure crisis and during COVID. The banks made out like bandits and had record years. I believe this can be a highly profitable investment while doing everything you can to serve borrowers well and help them as much as possible.

Others choose this strategy as a way to gain access to and control underlying assets as a type of backdoor channel, without having to compete in bidding wars when properties go on the market.

Others are drawn to mortgage debt for its passive income and ease of investing. You don't have any of the usual hassles of property ownership or tenants.

In the new normal and pandemic era, this is perhaps one of the best ways to be able to participate in optimal real estate locations, even when you can't or don't want to go there in person.

The Gotchas

While there are many advantages in this sector over direct investment in physical real estate assets, there are some extra things to learn before jumping in and trying to do it yourself.

Chief among them is knowing what you are buying and how to value notes. You need to have your finger on the pulse of the market and know what different types of notes are trading for.

You need to know how to evaluate note assets and perform your due diligence, such as lien and title searches and looking for quirks in the paperwork.

You must know how to handle issues such as bankruptcy and foreclosures, as well as ever-changing mortgage servicing rules.

As with any other investment opportunity, 99% of success is in execution and management. Here this means loan workouts, loan modifications, and responsive servicing. This can be an incredibly effective way to really do some meaningful good out there, or to just be yet another bad actor.

One gotcha that many aspiring mortgage note investors overlook is that while just about anyone can find a way to buy an individual note, or invest in a mortgage debt fund in some way, the best value and discounts are almost exclusively reserved for bigger buyers.

Think of this market like Costco for mortgage note investments. The real deals are often in bulk pools of notes that are sold in packages of millions, and even billions, of dollars. Just having that amount of cash isn't enough, either. A lot of regulation and responsibility exists on both sides. To even get a chance to bid on them, you need a very strong résumé, a credible track record, and proof that you can manage them well.

You may also have to make sense of that mix when you are buying a big pool, because it can be made up of different assets, types of debt, and performance levels.

Pro Tips for the Modern Intelligent Investor

A variety of types of debt and loans are available to invest in. Each has its own pros and cons. Each may line up slightly differently with your own strategy, goals, and timeline.

These include:

- Performing notes
- Nonperforming notes
- First lien mortgages
- Second lien mortgages
- Lines of credit
- Unsecured debt
- Residential mortgages
- Commercial mortgages
- Owner-occupied property
- Non-owner-occupied property

Performing Notes

These are loans that are being paid as agreed. The borrowers are on time with payments and haven't defaulted. These loans will typically trade at higher premiums and lower margins. They are a safer cash flow play.

Nonperforming Notes

These are loans on which borrowers haven't always paid as agreed. They may simply be late on mortgage payments, property taxes, or insurance premiums. They may have just fallen late, have rolling dates, or be in some stage of default.

There are also re-performing loans, or "scratch and dent loans," which don't have perfect payment history but can be current now; for example, if borrowers missed a couple of payments during a crisis but can make up the difference.

Typically, better discounts are available on these loans.

First Lien Mortgages

These are first-position loans, so they are the priority and first to be paid off in any refinance, sale, or foreclosure. Considered the least risky, these will have thinner margins than second liens.

Second Lien Mortgages

Loans in this category can be second mortgages or home equity lines of credit. There may also be third mortgages, or other debt secured by real estate.

Lines of Credit

Revolving lines of credit can be first or second liens on real estate. The main difference between these liens and other mortgage loans is that they are revolving lines of credit on which balances and payments fluctuate much more widely as borrowers use or pay down their lines.

Unsecured Debt

Unsecured debts that can be invested in include credit cards, personal loans and lines of credit, and business credit.

Residential Mortgages

These are loans on residential properties, such as one- to four-family homes and condos.

Commercial Mortgages

Commercial mortgage loans can cover loans on industrial, office, multi-family, retail, farmland, construction, and similar properties. Some investors prefer these notes due to less regulation and restrictions on foreclosing, so investors can move faster if borrowers fall late.

Owner-Occupied Property

Owner-occupied means the borrower lives in or uses the property. This could be a primary residence or a commercial property where the borrower runs their own business. Investors often prefer these loans because they believe borrowers will prioritize paying such a debt above others.

Non-Owner-Occupied Property

Non-owner-occupied means the borrower owns but does not live or work in a property full-time, such as investment homes, strip malls, etc. The advantage here can be cash flow coming in from rented units.

There can also be a big difference between judicial and nonjudicial states.

While the best notes can vary from month to month, there can be great advantages to having a strong mix in your portfolio: those that deliver the most reliable income, the best value and yields, and with lump-sum potential.

Again, the real difference is in the servicing and workouts, so employing a strong servicer who shares your values and can actually deliver on their best intentions is vital.

Until you get big enough and have been around long enough to get access to the best-value deals, it is probably smartest to partner with those who have the connections and résumé.

TAX LIENS

What it Is

Tax liens can often be overlooked and overhyped as an investment.

When a property owner fails to pay their annual property taxes on time, the county sells the debt to bidders at auction. This gives immediate cash to the county to cover their budget. Investors in tax liens are entitled to interest on the investment in the amount they bid. This can be up to 18%.

If the owner pays off the past-due taxes, then the investor gets their capital returned, along with the interest due.

If the owner does not pay, then the lien gives the investor a path to taking over ownership of the property for the amount of the debt.

Either way, you are going to get paid. It is just a matter of how much and how fast.

The Pros

The surety of getting paid and a return can be highly attractive to investors.

For many, this seems like the cheap route to getting started in real estate investing with little capital. While many treat it as a volume investment strategy, you can pick up individual liens very inexpensively. It is not uncommon to find tax liens for a couple of thousand dollars or less.

If you get to take a property this way, it becomes very cheap and highly profitable.

With more and more counties taking their tax lien sales and auctions online, this can also be a great way to invest out of your area remotely, and often with no hands-on management needed.

This niche can be highly attractive when other acquisition channels are too hot, competitive, and overpriced. If you are stumped on coming up with property or mortgage note deals, check out the temperature in this arena.

The Gotchas

One of the cons of tax lien investing is you don't exactly know how much the return will be, and when you are going to get your return of capital. This can make it trickier for individual investors who don't have a lot of flexibility, or who don't have a diverse portfolio with more certain asset allocation in income, growth, and various yield ranges.

There is a hard lockup period, too, in which these assets are pretty illiquid. It is short, but it is something to keep in mind.

While tax lien investing can sound like a low-capital, easy way to invest with miniscule risk, if you are hopping into auctions without knowing exactly what those assets are and any issues they may be facing, it can be less predictable than you think. A property could be mired in repair issues, code violations, litigation, and more.

The way this strategy has recently been sold through infomercials and online gurus has also meant that it can often be flooded with green investors who don't know what they are doing and bid far too much. When this happens, it can mean a lot of wasted time for more serious investors, unrealistic pricing, and periods when it just doesn't pay to engage in it.

In recent years, there also has been a lot of controversy about tax liens and tax auctions; the big issue being that some authorities have seized on the opportunity to use this channel to boost their income and revenues. Some consider this extremely predatory and abusive, especially when you consider that in some cases, they have seized homes for less than $100 and even less than $10 in past due taxes or missed fees, and have auctioned them off for a whole lot more.

In these potentially fraudulent and malicious cases, you might ask yourself if that is something you want to be involved in — stealing someone's home through no fault of their own. Fortunately, approached well, you may also find this as a way to do a whole lot of good and help people who have been robbed of their homes.

Pro Tips for the Modern Intelligent Investor

Tax liens can be a great part of your investment mix at certain moments in the cycle, although they are best executed at volume for even results and by experts who know their local markets intimately, down to the individual streets and properties.

You've got to know the moments to hop in and out of this space, and what makes a real deal.

NEW CONSTRUCTION

What it Is

Constructing properties of your own can be an incredibly exciting strategy for investors. It has certainly been one approach that has been the foundation of many billion-dollar companies, institutions, and funds.

You can choose to build anything from boutique townhome projects to entire single-family-home developments, mixed-use projects, commercial buildings, and multi-family apartments.

You can build from scratch and the ground up on virgin parcels of land, acquire prime properties, and tear down and replace out-of-date and functionally obsolete buildings.

The concept is creating something new and more valuable.

The Pros

One of the best benefits of new construction is being able to create your own inventory. When inventory is sparse, the market is too competitive for existing units, and asking prices just don't make sense, this is the way to keep money flowing in by creating your own deals.

At these moments, you can often build for a lot less than it costs to acquire an older existing unit.

You can build to rent or build to flip.

Although traditional single-family-home construction loans effectively evaporated after 2008, this strategy can benefit from leverage, whether through partners or having end users finance your build through preconstruction sales.

When you build your own inventory, you can also customize it for the market.

The Gotchas

New construction is hyper-risky. Speculative ("spec") building is probably the riskiest way to participate in real estate.

You must clearly and decisively differentiate between your creative hobbies and your investments. If you get caught up in making it pretty or building as if you were going to live there, you are going to lose a lot of money. Invest for profit first. Then you can build all the fun side projects you want to express your inner artist with your surplus cash.

When considering new construction as an investment, you must build for the market and customer. It is about solving a problem and filling an existing need, not a "build it and they will come" strategy.

If you've seen and been inspired by any of those extreme-home TV shows, remember that all those houses are empty. Millions of dollars were poured into those artistic architectural masterpieces, but they are vacant. No one is renting or living in them. Don't forget that.

These mistakes frequently bankrupt even the biggest organizations. You have to have a lot of financial cushion and reserve capital for these projects to attempt and profit from them.

This is not the fastest strategy. It may take up to two years to complete a project. In the meantime, many changes can occur, including in building codes, market conditions, rising material and labor costs, and shortages. If you haven't built in enough of a budget and spread to account for these things, it could get ugly. It's not easy to find a buyer for an incomplete construction project.

Pro Tips for the Modern Intelligent Investor

As with house-flipping and managing rentals, contractor management can make or break you in new construction. Without quality contractors, relationships, and expertise in managing them, it will be far more challenging.

Owning or maintaining tight control over contracting will be vital, especially when it comes to not getting caught short or getting crushed with inflation and labor shortages.

One of the great ways to de-risk this strategy and ensure you can benefit from the potential spreads and deal flow is to focus on preselling and pre-leasing: Have units sold or leased before you break ground.

CONVERSIONS

What it Is

Conversions are another powerful strategy for investors. This strategy isn't as common as some of the others on this list, yet it has huge potential. It can be one of the most significant investor plays when big shifts in markets occur.

A conversion is repurposing a building's use. Perhaps one of the most common examples is in condo conversions: taking an often-dated rental apartment building, converting the units to condos, and selling them off for big lump-sum gains. Converting industrial properties into residential ones is also popular.

It's about unlocking the maximum value from the highest and best use of an existing property in the current market.

In other phases of the market, when sales aren't as strong, it can make more sense to pull off a reverse conversion and take condos back to being rental units.

Given the massive transformational shifts that came out of the events of 2020–2022, even more properties may be ripe for conversion for the new era we are living and working in.

Repurposing retail and office buildings is probably the most obvious. Office space has become a pure luxury. According to the U.S. Energy Information Administration, the U.S. had 97 billion square feet of commercial space back in 2018. If 23% of that is office space, there may now easily be 25 billion square feet of unnecessary office space in America — while there seems to be significant shortages in housing.

Those buildings can be converted into condos or rental apartments, or even industrial, warehouse, and self-storage space.

The Pros

This strategy is about finding, adding, and extracting value, and at scale.

It can be faster and less intensive than completely new ground-up construction, meaning a faster turnaround on investments and increased profitability from the economies of scale involved.

The Gotchas

These deals can sometimes rely on all units agreeing to the conversion, which isn't always simple and can take some great sales skills.

Rezoning may be required in some cases, and that can take time and money, too, and sometimes even political influence.

If you aren't quick enough, then the market can change back the other way on you, too.

Pro Tips for the Modern Intelligent Investor

Conversions can be a strategic way to scale up what you are doing and find sweet spots in the market.

To avoid getting caught by changing factors, be sure to maintain flexibility and multiple exit strategies.

Try to get buy-in from all parties in a decision in advance, and be sure you have a strong legal team to guide you through it.

YOUR OWN FUND

What it Is

Another increasingly interesting investment alternative for serious and scaling investors is to create their own funds. (I've written more about doing this in my previous books if that is a path you are considering taking.)

It means pooling investment capital together that you can then invest in more assets.

Most funds have traditionally focused on one niche, because that is about all they can handle —for example, the office sector, mobile home parks, rental apartments, or mortgage debt.

You aim to make such superior returns that you can pay an attractive enough yield to your investors and still have enough left to earn some attractive fees or spread on top of that.

The Pros

As a fund, you are able to operate at greater economies of scale than on your own. Variations of this can be multi-family, offices, and partnerships in REITs.

It is a move designed to get you into bigger deals and gain more access, better discounts and yields, and clout in operations that you can't achieve alone.

The Gotchas

The main gotchas here are that most such funds don't fully appreciate until their creators are deep into them and the enormous amount of extra work on all sides of this equation.

You now not only have all the work of finding, vetting, acquiring, and managing investments at a far larger scale than before, but also finding — and more importantly, managing — your new investors. That alone is a full-time job for a whole team.

Investor management is far more intensive than you can imagine; far more so if you are going to deliver great, responsive service that will retain your investors and result in referrals and repeat investments.

Too much capital can be a concern, too. Once you take that money from your investors, you have a huge responsibility to invest it, make it work, protect it, and derive great returns with it. You've got to find the deals and deploy the capital. This challenge is why you sometimes see big funds ultimately settling for terrible yields or far overpaying for assets. They are under a lot of pressure.

Pro Tips for the Modern Intelligent Investor

Fund managers who are aces at balancing all sides at the top of the game and for long periods of time are far more rare than celebrity athletes. Think more like Steve Jobs-level rare.

The silver bullet for this is to focus your time and energy and invest in becoming an expert on one side of the equation. The easiest is probably raising the capital. Then, through arbitrage, invest the capital you raise in a more established, proven fund that will do all the hard work. You get a slice, with a lot less work and stress, while you get even better at raising the capital.

Chapter 3

THE #1 TRAP REAL ESTATE INVESTORS FALL INTO

What do you think is the number one mistake that investors make?

There can be lots of little ones, but if there is one thing that takes investors out of the game more than others, even if they get everything else right, what do you think it is?

Overpaying for assets, picking subpar tenants, underestimating project costs, and holding a little too long can all be painful blunders. As a one-off mistake that is part of a much bigger portfolio, those may not be fatal, although they can be for smaller investors.

However, failing to diversify is a critical flaw that will catch up to everyone sooner or later. When it does, it is devastating. It will destroy even those with billions of dollars in investments or under management, who have had insane surpluses and seemed like geniuses for a while.

Let's look at some of the ways lack of diversity leads to catastrophic failure.

STRATEGIC FAILURE

Only having one strategy is a sure way to destine yourself to financial failure.

Perhaps this irks you, too. You see one self-proclaimed guru after another popping up online or on TV. Every one of them pushes the fact that they have the one and only way to invest, or the only right way to invest. They dismiss everything else. Perhaps their thing is tax liens or flipping houses or rentals. It stinks, and perhaps one day, it may become a legal issue.

The truth is that all the investment strategies we have covered do work — if you work them well. You can do very well in each of these sectors and niches. Sadly, these gurus are often newbies themselves. They haven't been around long enough to experience the issues and flaws in their own single-minded strategies.

It has been said that you may be able to fool some people for quite a while. You may even be able to fool everyone for a moment. But you can't fool everyone forever. The truth is going to come out. Unfortunately, it is usually in a very painful and costly way.

Anyone can have or be a one-hit wonder. Anyone can find 15 minutes of fame. Some have strong streaks. Even a complete amateur can get in on a bull run with almost zero understanding of what they are doing and look like King Midas — but remember what happened to him. It just doesn't last.

I've admittedly been there myself. I ran into this wall hard in 2008. It took me awhile before I could drag myself out of bed. I don't want you to have to experience that. If you have, then this book is all about sharing the solution that has worked for me in the wake of it.

Can you imagine an athlete who only had one move, one play?

This is why all UFC fighters now train in all styles, even if they have a strong suit. They eventually figured out that if you are only good at standing up, you will be obliterated in milliseconds when you get taken to the ground. No matter how big or strong they are, and how many title belts they had before. The same is true of those with a great ground game. You can't just lie on the floor when the starting bell rings and hope the other guy or girl comes over and lies down so that you have a shot, right? No, they are just going to stomp you on the ground, and it's over.

Just like a basketball player can't play with only one shot, it wouldn't work. If you are in the NFL, you can't only have one play. After the first couple of plays, you will be demolished by everyone you play, every time, until you are out of the league.

Countless examples of this exist, such as office leasing. Someone who was making billions in office leasing in December 2019 had zero income and was looking for a new job by the first quarter of 2020, when COVID showed up (unless they also happened to be selling office buildings or leasing houses to the 40% of Manhattan's population who fled the city).

It's like saying you still only accept money in the form of a paper check. Most people today don't even know what those are, let alone have ever held one or know how to write one.

Every real estate investment strategy can work super-well if done right. Virtually all these strategies will continue to work into infinity, although they won't always work on the same level of performance each month. They also each have their own place for producing different types of results.

You have to have that, too. If someone came along and said they wanted to give you $10M in one lump sum, you wouldn't turn it down because you insisted on only taking it in monthly payments for the next 10 years, would you? Or how about the opposite?

Being blinded by only having a recession-viable strategy versus one that optimizes for bull runs, one that only generates lump sums versus monthly cash flow, or one that is only preservation-focused versus a grow-at-all-costs mentality isn't going to help you. It won't get you what you really want over time.

You need all of these as a part of a sound and prosperous portfolio and functional financial plan.

Recession Proofing vs. Bull Run Strategies

If your money isn't protected before a recession, you can lose everything virtually overnight. I've seen it firsthand. It doesn't matter how famous or rich you might be today, no one is immune to it.

At the same time, when it is raining real estate gold out there, it's smart to put out a big bucket and capture as much of it as you can. Otherwise, during these times, hyperinflation can be almost as damaging as a recession and a nose-diving market.

If you sit on the fences in the good times, you'll miss out on a ton of growth. While you can find great value and discounts in down markets, it will be hard to keep up financially if you aren't participating in the runs, too.

Lump-Sum Gains vs. Cash Flow

Receiving passive income cash flow from your investments is critical. Without it, the countdown to bankruptcy is on and ticking fast, regardless of whether you just won the lottery, signed a multi-million-dollar work contract, or inherited a sizable fortune.

You *must* have your money working for you. You *must* have cash flow.

Can you imagine having a $2B yacht or $20M home, and then losing it because you were short of the cash for maintenance!

At the same time, it is true that this type of investment typically feeds you cash more slowly than lump sum-generating investments, such as renting out a home versus flipping one.

Both feed each other and ensure your success. Lump-sum gains can facilitate other investments, provide the ability to take advantage of opportunities, and fill gaps when hiccups occur in your anticipated cash flow. Just think of COVID.

In turn, that regular cash flow can make all the difference in being able to see those opportunities through and receiving their maximum rewards.

Wealth Preservation vs. Rapid Growth

If you don't preserve your capital, then you may have nothing to invest and make gains or generate income with. However, if you are too conservative, such as making 4% yields before taxes and fees, you might be in the hole at the end of each year, especially when inflation is on the rise. You may have a net negative yield.

At the same time, a growth-at-all-costs approach is almost always fatal in the end. We've seen this be the Achilles heel of $40B companies. You have to protect your gains as you grow or it will all implode. You will stretch yourself too thin, with no support for any unexpected flinches in markets or glitches in life.

The classic example of this mistake is having only a five-year plan: just trying to survive the moment, or thinking you can rush and make all the money you'll ever need if you go all out for the next five years. The problem comes when those five years are up. You might have blown through all your goals, but set yourself up for imminent financial disaster.

This is where knowing your two ROIs is so important. Yes, first you need to invest for the Return *of* Investment. That is getting your capital back. The Return *on* Investment, or gains, come second to that, although they cannot be ignored or you are at risk of devaluing your capital.

You need downside protection *and* growth in your portfolio.

GEOGRAPHIC CONFINEMENT

If you are really bold, you may be dreaming of building a real estate empire — owning every building you can see from your window, or being able to drive down the street and point out how much of it you own. That can feel great. Density can have benefits. Within reason.

You may be investing only locally out of fear. Perhaps you are afraid to get pro help with investing beyond your city, state, or country, so you stay within reach of what you can drive to every day, staying just within your comfort bubble. Again, there can be advantages to investing within your circle of competence and what you know best.

Yet, in both of these scenarios, being confined to one geographic area is almost always a fatal mistake, eventually.

Obvious examples of this exist, such as areas prone to hurricanes and wildfires — like living on the side of a volcano, it's not a matter of if you'll be affected, it is just a matter of when, and how badly.

Real estate and mortgage investors have many ways to minimize their risks from these situations, both directly at the physical property level — think hurricane shutters and building well above flood levels — as well as layers of insurance that can cover any financial losses. Still, the disruption can be painful.

If this happens to one property in your personal portfolio in a given year, it is typically not a big deal. Your other assets will cover your income and financial needs. If your portfolio is in 100 units, and one of them gets wiped out, you'll probably be fine if you miss out on a 100th of your income for a couple of months.

In contrast, it doesn't matter if you have one or 1,000 properties in your portfolio if they are all in the same area, and they are all wiped out in one fire or storm. You'll probably have no income coming in, and perhaps little equity or liquidity to repair those assets or cover costs while waiting for insurance payouts.

This can play out the same if you only have a 400-unit waterfront condo building in Miami or own the entire city of New Orleans.

In addition to these more high-profile risks, others can be just as severe, but often fly under the radar of most investors.

Local politics and regulations can be a risk, such as rent regulation, business and investor environments, eviction rules, and taxes. Some jurisdictions have long had consistent themes and directions in these trends. New York and California are two of the most obvious.

These factors can be amplified and accelerated during events like COVID. The directions that states like California and New York have taken have been night-and-day different from those like Florida and Texas.

You have a vote and can be involved in the decision-making process, even though you may not be able to control everything. Geographic diversification can help you mitigate and minimize the potential impacts of these risks.

Different markets rotate at different times in the economic and real estate cycle, too. Geographic diversity can help smooth this out and keep you ahead of the curve.

VOLUME OF ASSETS VS. THE ROULETTE WHEEL MINDSET

If you think that going to Las Vegas, finding the first roulette wheel you can, and throwing everything you have "all on black" is investing, then you can skip this section.

Ironically, many investors fall into this approach without really thinking about it. This can especially be a risk for new investors who are starting out. They try to go it alone and throw everything into one deal. It's not much better than playing roulette.

Compare that to having even a piece of 10 or 100 or 1,000 properties instead. Your odds of success are far better. Your chances of success are more like "the house," which always wins, versus the individual player, who always has the odds stacked against them. Compounded, this advantage is benefiting from the many economies of scale in your portfolio.

Chapter 4

TIMELESS INVESTMENT PRINCIPLES

While new trends, technologies, and even strategies shouldn't be ignored and can provide an edge, timeless investment principles shouldn't be dismissed on the way.

This does not mean being stuck in the status quo. These timeless investment principles have proved to be invaluable for financial success for at least decades, if not centuries and thousands of years. They've built and protected the wealthiest investors in our history. Breaking them has always ended up proving to be financially catastrophic. They can be directly traced to making the difference between the wealthy and everyone else.

These principles are so important that I have a whole new book in the works dedicated just to these foundational investment principles.

Here are just some of these concepts that will always be pivotal:

- Don't lose money.
- Expect volatility and profit from it.
- Don't be fooled into thinking you can time the market perfectly.

- Invest regularly and consistently.
- Investing is best when it is most businesslike.
- It's not what you make, but what you get to keep that matters.
- Understand what you are investing in.
- Every investment should have a purpose.
- Failing to plan is planning to fail.
- Don't blindly follow the herd.
- Fortune favors those who take action.
- Diversification.
- Location, location, location.

TIMELESS INVESTMENT PRINCIPLES

Don't Lose Money

Intelligent diversification will enable you to avoid losing money. It limits and insulates against losses. It also ensures that the money you need is there and available when you need it.

It means achieving true diversification, as well as being sure your money is being active — working for you, rather than staying idle and being eaten away by inflation and the devaluation of money.

Expect Volatility & Profit from it

Change is always happening. Some markets move much faster than others, so volatility is always a factor. Ignoring that will cost you dearly, if you underestimate the speed at which it can happen or the drag caused by appreciation that is too slow.

Volatility in itself is not a risk, but an opportunity, as long as you understand it, and focus on smart investments versus speculating.

Be sure your portfolio empowers you to benefit from volatility, in buying low and profiting from appreciation, while protecting you from deep dips or underperforming investments.

Don't Be Fooled into Thinking You Can Time the Market Perfectly

Yes, intelligent and experienced investors are equipped to spot trends and cycles and know the leading indicators and patterns of shifting markets. Still, even the best acknowledge that they are not perfect at timing the markets.

There are always wild cards — crises like pandemics and wars, and market manipulation through large trades and the media can make markets behave differently from what the fundamentals suggest they should. At least in the short term.

Investors have to be very careful to keep their egos in check, as well as to avoid and watch out for clichéd one-liners that often indicate a change is coming: "It's different this time," or "We've got another 12 to 18 months."

It is always better to err on the side of buying early and selling early.

Invest Regularly & Consistently

One of the best principles to ensure that you are maintaining performance and traction over time is the discipline to continue to invest regularly and consistently.

This adds more objectivity and minimizes the impact of emotional investing, or getting your market timing wrong.

You'll not only be investing in a more varied lineup of assets, but also diversifying your buy-in positions and your potential gains or exposure to losses.

Investing Is Best When it Is Most Businesslike

It is great to be passionate about your work and what you invest in, but the best investments are not emotional decisions. They are objective, fact-based, numbers-driven, and executed on professionally.

Your investing should be organized, managed in a businesslike way, and focused on the data, with experienced human intelligence.

This will save you from going all in on the wrong things, holding assets for too long, and experiencing excess liability in holding and operating them.

It's Not What You Make, But What You Get to Keep that Matters

The top line is irrelevant unless you are only competing with others on that for vanity reasons. Building net income and wealth is about how much you get to keep.

Fees, uncalculated costs, and taxes can all take a huge bite out of your real results. This factor alone can make a huge difference in what you can add to your portfolio and how you can generate more profitability from some assets than others.

In addition to the financials, this also affects how much time and quality of life you have outside of your work and investing. Be sure you are diversifying with these factors in mind as well.

If you are putting everything into your own business, you can make yourself time- and health-poor.

Understand What You Are Investing in

Diversifying into varied asset classes can be wise and profitable — but it is also important to have some understanding of what you are investing in. At least the fundamentals. What makes value? What kills it? What factors influence the performance of a given asset class?

If you deeply understand biotech, and the underlying medicine, technology, and companies, then maybe you want a piece of that. If you really understand the value and levers of a certain NFT, then it may be a fun bet. The same goes for cryptocurrencies.

Just doing it because everyone else is doing it is not a good investment strategy.

The great thing about real estate is that most investors are familiar with it. If you've rented an apartment or bought a home, you already understand some of the basic fundamentals, such as price, experience, competition, etc.

It is also much easier to track various factors and trends in real estate than other sectors. You can quickly get a rough handle on new areas to diversify into. Take a vacation somewhere of interest for a long weekend and talk to people, and you'll find out a lot about the dynamics and market of that area.

Perhaps even more importantly, this is about knowing who you are investing with. Focus on vetting and picking the right advisors who know their stuff, and you don't have to sweat getting all the minute details down to each screw in each investment. Fail to pick them well, and it doesn't matter how great the opportunity or market fundamentals. They can still blow it.

Every Investment Should Have a Purpose

When planning your diversification, it is important to have a purpose for each investment and new step that you make.

Wild, unfocused diversification will kill you just as fast as no diversification at all.

Each investment should have a specific purpose. That may be by category, such as passive income, growth, or wealth preservation, recession proofing, and so on. It may be even more specific, such as specific investments to cover certain needs and goals — college tuition, taking care of aging parents, annual vacations, etc.

This way, your diversification will actually deliver on what you want. Otherwise, investing for the sake of it probably won't give you what you hope for when you need the money, or when it comes to retiring or your legacy.

Failing to Plan Is Planning to Fail

Successful investing and diversification require some planning — at least some level of basic planning and guidance about what you want, and what you need to be investing in to get it. This includes:

- Clarity on your goals
- Creating a sustainable plan
- Planning for market changes
- Succession planning
- Accounting for the unexpected
- Tax strategies and moves
- Planning your investment contributions

This process will also ensure you don't get bogged down in debating about making investments, and ultimately miss out on important trades.

Don't Blindly Follow the Herd

Some benefits can exist to taking advantage of the herd mentality and profiting from trends and runs — as long as you are hedging against the moment the herd stampedes right off the cliff into the financial trap that has been set for them.

Of course, most of the greatest wealth and leaps in finances have been made through contrarian investing and betting against the herd. You can diversify to make the best of both strategies simultaneously.

Fortune Favors Those Who Take Action

All the planning, great ideas, smart strategies, and intentions are worth nothing without real action.

Theory is for the classroom and getting good grades in school. If you want to take your daydreams to reality, then you have to start making investments.

Diversification

Perhaps most pivotal and important of all is the principle of diversification.

You can get a lot of things wrong and still survive by applying this timeless investment principle. Just as you can seem to get everything right on some investments, and still end up bankrupt due to a lack of diversification. It really makes that much difference.

In fact, diversifying alone can help you win on virtually all these other timeless investment principles. It will help you not to lose money. To survive and thrive despite volatility, invest objectively instead of emotionally, and get far more reliable results.

You may have heard some people say that the key to success in real estate is "location, location, location." The overarching umbrella for success in investing above that is to *"diversify, diversify, diversify."*

As we'll touch on in an upcoming chapter about knowing your endgame instead of taking the common path of starting by striking out to look for a great investment, it may be wisest and most profitable to first think about and lay out a plan for how you will diversify your finances.

To create a sound financial plan and portfolio, lay out the different results or factors you need to attain. What does that asset allocation mix look like? How will you begin investing across this board from the start, instead of ending up in the weeds in one thing and hoping you can branch out later?

Just to drive home how important this is, and that it can touch everyone and anyone, let's take a quick look at some examples of major losses, and how diversification may have saved the day for both the brightest billionaires and money managers, as well as millions of average individuals.

WeWork is an example of one of both the greatest success stories and most horrific failures. The office leasing tech startup soared to a $47B valuation and found backing from some of the world's most notable investment firms, like SoftBank.

Then, just before their IPO, the cracks opened, and in just 30 days, they were on the verge of bankruptcy, losing their investors tens of billions of dollars, almost overnight.

This shouldn't have been a huge surprise. While there were a lot of great things about co-working and the original WeWork, there were obvious fatal flaws in their model and the way they leveraged themselves up in subleasing.

They became so much of a risk that no one wanted to lease them more space to fuel their growth, and investors backed away. When insane growth and debt is your only way to stay afloat, any blip or stall will be devastating.

They could have avoided that pain and loss for everyone involved with better diversification.

Then you have fund manager Bill Ackman and his fall from grace in the Valeant debacle. This famous money manager managed to lose his investors around $4B almost overnight in one bad play. According to Bloomberg, investors were still out billions of dollars years later.

Interestingly, Ackman chose to take his own money that he made from putting others into these stocks and investments and put it into personal real estate investments. Like the $100M penthouse he bought to flip, with the hopes of reselling it for $500M. In this case, too much in one big bet was a disaster for many investors. Yet he personally leveraged diversification to survive financially himself.

Warren Buffett is another example. While some see him as a magical picker of investments, even he admits he is terrible at trying to time the market. Instead, he focuses on the value and performance of each individual investment, so he has diversified broadly while counting real estate as his best investments. In fact, his investments in mobile homes and mortgage loans enabled him and his investment company to survive through the 2008 crisis.

Then there is multi-billionaire Sam Zell. He started investing in multi-family apartments while in school, then branched out to commercial property and retirement communities, and even homes in Mexico. He became famous for buying up properties dirt cheap, for as little as a dollar in crisis times, and finding great exits to huge Wall Street funds, right before market crashes.

I've learned a lot through the years, too, such as how to stay diversified to deliver consistent results all the time, while anticipating market changes and being prepared to take advantage of volatility. As I started out in business, I also learned a lot about the *wrong* ways to diversify, such as being too diversified into businesses and investments that were too varied.

Location, Location, Location

We'll dig deeper into location and what it means for your investing and diversification in another chapter, including prime; ultra prime; and what's trendy versus actual returns, fundamentals, and your goals.

This brings us to our next chapter and how to master this delicate balance for ongoing success.

Chapter 5

DIVERSIFICATION VS. FOCUS

Perhaps the most important and valuable lesson I've learned over the past two decades of investing, participating in real estate and debt markets, and operating businesses is the necessity to balance diversification with focus and specialization.

Some of the first books I read about money and investing taught me a lot about the value of diversification and multiple streams of income. There is a lot of wisdom in that. Both are vital. Yet I've learned there are better ways to do it. There are cons in being too broad.

If you've read my previous books, you know how I began applying the concepts of diversification and multiple streams of income by branching out into different types of businesses. House-flipping, salons, car washes, you name it. The multiple streams of income and diversity were good. Yet it also meant trying to master, or perhaps not truly mastering, these very different industries — at least not to the level of someone whose only life focus and decades of expertise were in those fields. I took a lot of knowledge transfer, general business acumen, and skills that could cross over from those businesses, but I may not have been the best expert in the salon or car wash industry there ever was.

Trying to master all sides of multiple businesses, each of which could be a career or calling on its own, makes the advantages of specialization clear. This is true as a professional, business owner, and investor.

THE BENEFITS OF SPECIALIZATION

We all see the benefits and advantages of specialization around us every day. From the most basic perspective, we can see it in just about every job and role.

Even if you've never had a traditional job and jumped right into entrepreneurship, you've seen it. Even if you've just had an after-school or summer job at a fast-food restaurant, you've seen it. When you started out, there was someone who landed the best job roles and titles, could get the same things done a lot faster than everyone else, instinctively understood where an issue was, and knew the right questions to ask. People looked up to them. People relied on their input for solutions. As a result, they got paid a lot better than everyone else. In some cases, you may have had someone like this walk into your company and be given a lot of freedom, power, and authority — because they brought a lot of specialization, education, and experience with them.

We are constantly seeking out specialists in our daily lives, too. It's true whether we've recognized it and done it consciously or not.

This is true almost without exception. Unless we are in a dire financial pinch, and the lowest-cost thrift store solution is the only option. Otherwise, we appreciate the value of specialization.

Even with the most basic items, we appreciate and most of us gravitate toward specialization. Not many people go to McDonald's just for a coffee. People go to places like Starbucks for that. We like to go to specialists when it comes time to go out to eat, and having a good meal experience is important. If you were going out on a date or for an anniversary or important business meal, you'd gravitate toward a restaurant known for its specialist chef, who really knows their stuff. You wouldn't pick up sushi from Walmart.

If you were traveling to a new country and going off the beaten path into the jungle or the desert, or to climb a mountain, you'd want a specialist guide, right?

When it comes to getting our information, we look to experts in their fields, even if information is available in the news.

This is especially true in business and with our money. Even if you are just selling your own home, you'd probably look for a Realtor who is the neighborhood expert, right? If you run a business, you want a marketing expert to run your promotions and publicity. You want a CPA to handle your record keeping and taxes. If you end up in a legal situation, you want an experienced lawyer who practices in that field, whether it is a tax, corporate, trademark, or family law matter. And so on.

When it comes to being the specialist, there are many advantages. Here are just some of them.

Relationships, Connections, & Access

The best connections, relationships, and access only come with time and specialization.

People at the top of the game in every field tend to flock together. This is true of billionaires, scientists, and so on. Their time is their most valuable asset. They guard it well. They prize spending it with those they can also learn from. To get access to these circles, their wisdom, and their connections takes either being a specialist yourself or having a lot of money. Often it takes both.

Access to the best deals, decision-makers, and opportunities often only comes with specialization. Especially when it comes to things like mortgage notes or REOs, you have to have a strong résumé, built over years, with many zeros on it. Specialization means a credible reputation in your field.

This isn't just about what specialization does for you individually, but the value that access enables you to pass on to others as well.

In my case, this means the access I have earned in terms of big pools of real estate and debt assets — the best deals on them are something I get to share and pass on to my partners, investors, and clients, and their clients. It is value they can't access yet themselves.

You may be the best heart surgeon, lawyer, or basketball player, but unless you give all that up and spend the next 20 years in real estate full-time, you probably won't ever get access to the best investments, on the best terms, on your own. Fortunately, by leveraging the expertise and access of others, you can hack your way in.

I know that if I have a heart issue or legal issue, or bet on sports, I'd lean on a specialist. It doesn't matter how much I need it; even if I put in 20 years in medical school or law school starting now, I may never be that specialist. I certainly probably couldn't master it in time for my needs.

Most people out there can't wait 20 years to invest after mastering an area, either.

On the other side, this also means attracting the best talent and specialists in other fields to want to work for you, such as marketing pros, salespeople, servicers, financiers, and so on.

Enhanced ROI on Everything You Do

The more of a specialist you are, the better you can perform, and the more efficiently you'll operate on all fronts.

You'll operate with more ease and confidence when you operate in your zone of expertise.

You'll be able to achieve more elite levels of performance than if you were spread thin. Sports is a great analogy for this. Whether it is soccer, basketball, or the NFL, players have diverged to play very different roles. A forward in soccer probably can't become an effective goalkeeper on the fly in a championship game. They've practiced shooting for tens of thousands of hours. The goalkeeper has spent those thousands of hours blocking shots. In American football, there are many specialist roles. Would the quarterback be as good at their job if they played as a defensive lineman, running back, or kicker every other game?

Specialization means a better ROI on everything you do. Someone who practices shooting baskets all day has much higher odds of scoring when they throw than someone who only practices once a month for an hour or so at a time, right?

When it comes to business and investing, your expertise means you will get a lot better results from each of your marketing campaigns, acquisition offers, fundraising campaigns, workout efforts, leasing campaigns, etc.

That ROI across the board compounds to be pretty formidable when it comes to results.

Risk Awareness

With specialization comes greater awareness of risk. Especially when it comes to real estate and finance, it takes years to understand all the risks, nuances, and glitches that can happen. No one can possibly get it all in an online course, a weekend seminar, or even a $40,000 coaching program or studying for a master's degree. There is just so much that only comes with doing a high volume of deals, over a long period of time, to uncover all these risks and potential challenges.

Equipped with that hindsight, you can then spot the issues before they arise, and know the questions to ask in advance and how to avoid the mistakes.

This not only makes the difference in millions of dollars and many percentage points in net returns, but in bankruptcy and profitability, too. It only takes one big blunder to fall hard into the red in this business.

Valuable Insights

On the other side of this coin, the specialist knows how to spot and unlock value that others don't see. Too many people end up passing on incredible opportunities because they don't understand the hidden value, or how to extract the most value out of assets and deals. When you specialize, you can see the whole matrix.

This is just like a medical specialist who knows all the potential things to look for and test for, potential prescription interactions, complications, and how to do things the rest of us don't.

You can see changes coming before 90% of everyone else, and prepare to win on that information.

THE DISADVANTAGES OF SPECIALIZATION

There are some disadvantages of specializing too much.

Limited Sources of Income

This may be true for chefs, farmers, physicians, and attorneys: If you were one of those stop-foreclosure attorneys in 2009, you had to find a whole other line of business shortly after that. Wheat farmers have been pummeled since so many people went gluten-free. If you were a doctor who only made money from in-person checkups in 2019, you had zero income when COVID restrictions came along.

This applies to everyone, and perhaps even more so for investors and business owners.

If there is one thing everyone should have learned from COVID, if not Facebook blackouts and ad fraud, or the 2008 financial crisis, it should be that everyone needs multiple streams of income. Even better, multiple streams of *passive* income.

Tunnel Vision

One of the biggest and most common dangers of being too narrowly focused is suffering from tunnel vision. It's inevitable — biological science — unless you've planned to hack your way out of it in advance.

The Eye Institute says that tunnel vision is "when your peripheral or 'side' vision deteriorates, or is lost altogether. The result is that you may only be able to see things in a small circle directly in front of your eyes." *Medical News Today* says it can be "serious and require medical attention as soon as possible to help prevent further damage."

Texting while driving is another example of this, and why it is so bad. We all know the tragic results that it leads to. The same applies to our finances. It can be catastrophic.

In investing, tunnel vision often ends up meaning you find yourself in a deep hole. You get caught by changing markets, macro changes, and lack of diversification. You don't have other perspectives and the flexibility to ride that out well without taking a loss. It takes too long to correct and adjust if you are just reacting rather than having been proactive. You'll often keep on flogging the horse long after it's dead.

You'll also miss out on the great upswings happening elsewhere in the markets — you'll lose a lot more in the dips than others, and you'll miss out on the bull runs that could offset or lift you out of that.

Better diversification in your investments provides a much better and more accurate, well-rounded view of what's happening. You will intrinsically see the whole macro picture, influences in the market, trends coming down the pipe, and real data versus manipulated media stats.

In real estate, for example, this might help you identify that a leading indicator market like Miami or Manhattan is beginning to decline, giving you extra lead time for your investing in the Midwest or in more suburban and rural areas.

You may see mortgage defaults increasing in the shadows, or the turnaround, when you can buy assets at better prices that are already poised for the upswing.

You can shift your investments and dollars more easily to what will be performing better, and limit your downside exposure without much effort or cost.

Stuck in the Status Quo

Overspecializing can also cause you to be stuck in the status quo. If you are just doing the same thing, and the same thing as other investors, you can only get mediocre, average results.

That's not going to be enough to get or keep you ahead.

This doesn't just apply to individual or mom-and-pop investors either. Even the largest corporations and banks have fallen victim to this.

The Cons of Traditional Diversification

While there are certainly some timeless money and investment principles that you should cling to, there are also outdated or "traditional" techniques that no longer work well or in your favor.

Some things may not belong in your investment portfolio or financial plan at all anymore. Some should be substantially minimized.

Outdated methods of thinking and portfolio diversification may look something like:

- Public stocks
- Funds of funds in public stocks
- Bonds
- Precious metals
- Money market accounts or CDs
- Your home

Chances are you are not following bonds, what their underlying fundamentals are, how much they have changed — or how you may end up in a negative yield situation once you factor in fees, taxes, and inflation.

If you default-invested in the stock market, you are probably spread across dozens of, if not 100 or more, stocks, that you really don't understand. You don't know what the fundamentals are or what influences their movement, and you have zero control over their value. It's just investing blind, "because everyone else was doing it." There is no true diversification, because when the stock market crashes, it crashes hard across the board, with no downside protection. It's an emotionally driven roller coaster. Note that this definitely applies to publicly traded stocks of real estate sector companies, too.

Gold and cash-like ways to park your money may not work the way they used to when your parents invested in them. You've got to have a reason to do it. You've got to know why you are doing it, and why it is better than other investment choices. Maybe they are not.

Those who think their own home is their investment in real estate are sorely underexposed to this asset class.

In a nutshell, dramatically broad diversification just for the sake of it will probably severely underserve you. At best, it will give you average results — and as we know, average is usually just broke.

HOW TO BALANCE BOTH DIVERSIFICATION & SPECIALIZATION

Diversification is essential and specialization can be hugely helpful. Yet there are also ugly pitfalls and dire financial side effects of going too far off the deep end in either direction.

This leaves one critical question: how to effectively balance both diversification and focus for the best possible results?

After first diving into a variety of different types of businesses, and then individually specializing in various real estate-related sectors, I've since found it possible to get the optimal results from diversifying under the same area of focus. Then simplifying how investors can participate in achieving similar results.

Wouldn't it be great if you could combine all the positives of focus and diversification into one investment? And with real estate?

That is now possible. Before we get into that, though, we'll take a look at some of the important different types of diversification that you need and want in your portfolio, and why.

Still, while we are on the topic, this principle of simplicity in diversifying is key. You can put a penny into a thousand different stocks. But then, to be investing wisely, you probably need to learn a ton about everything from biotech and pharmaceuticals to the food chain, to fossil fuels and how cars are made and sold, to the ins and outs of IPOs, and so much more. There may only be a handful of people on the planet who can do all of that well, if that.

A little more focus will help you make far better investments. Never mind the ROI on your time.

Then there are the costs associated with diversification. Aside from learning time and researching, there is time associated with making many transactions. If you could make 10, five, or just one transaction instead of 100, there are certainly financial savings on your time.

Then consider transaction fees. There may be setup fees, and even exit fees for some investments. Don't overlook this math — it affects your net. A few dollars a trade may not sound like much, but when you are making 100 trades, it adds up fast. In direct real estate investments, transaction fees can be thousands, tens of thousands, and easily six figures or more when doing it yourself (obviously, depending on what you are buying and selling). You may make a whole lot more per transaction, but ignoring these double-sided transaction costs means inaccurately calculating your true gains and ROI.

Chapter 6

DEEP & BROAD DIVERSIFICATION

There is more than one type of diversification. To be successful, we need both deep and broad diversification, within boundaries that keep it profitable.

These are some of the ways that you can diversify within the real estate sector. Some are obvious. Others you may not have thought about or realized were so important and pivotal.

INVESTMENT STRATEGIES

Earlier in this book, we covered some of the most common real estate investment-related strategies, their pros and cons, and some pro tips. Now, let's briefly touch on them again from a diversification perspective and the roles they can play in your intelligent portfolio.

Property Flipping

Flipping can produce lump sums of cash in the short term. Short hold times mean lower risk. Chunks of capital mean liquidity, wealth growth, and the ability to quickly restructure your portfolio for new opportunities if needed.

Value-add strategies also give investors more power to drive great returns in all phases of the market and economy.

Buy & Hold Income Properties

This is all about more consistent returns over the medium to long term in your portfolio. It also provides passive income and cash flow.

Secondary to this, these assets can provide wealth preservation and organic appreciation. Providing a hedge against inflation and tax benefits are other top reasons that intelligent investors put these assets into their portfolios.

Mortgage Debt Investing

The most obvious reason to put these assets in your portfolio is for cash flow and passive income, along with having hard assets to provide security at the same time.

However, there are also variants of this strategy that focus more on value-add or opportunistic investment for wealth gains. Others put a higher priority on consistency in performance and income.

Some of the options in this sector and the primary benefit include:

- Performing mortgage notes: predictable cash flow and yields
- Nonperforming mortgage notes: wealth gains and higher yields
- Second mortgages: higher yields
- Private lending: high yields and security

PROPERTY TYPES

Different property types can also add more diversification to your portfolio.

Residential One- to Four-Family Homes

This is the bread and butter of the industry — the most liquid and plentiful property type. Often the easiest to buy and sell, with lots of flexibility. Flip them or hold them.

Condos, Etc.

Condos, co-ops, townhomes, and "aparthotel" units are sometimes dumped into this category. However, some substantial differences exist.

Individual condos and townhomes are typically part of associations. Condo and homeowner associations can certainly complicate things. Profitable deals can be found. However, leasing, financing these deals, and selling them can be trickier. Associations have a lot of power over granting these activities, or restricting and blocking them. Mortgage lenders will look hard at the association and the makeup of its owners. These units often aren't as easy to rent or resell. A lot will be out of your control.

Co-ops are typically even more complicated. Lenders do not like these properties. Instead of actually buying and owning a piece of the actual real estate or physical unit, you are only buying shares in an entity, which in turn owns the building. It's more like a stock than investing in real estate.

Condotels & Aparthotels

These are a very unique type of real estate. They have sometimes grown in popularity in certain phases of the market and in popular vacation spots. A hotel-like building can be split into both partially owner-occupied, or second home and vacation units, and hotel rooms. Or owners may get a couple of weeks a year in their own unit, and then have the hotel manage it the rest of the year.

Again, financing can be a big issue for accessing capital or reselling and exiting investments. The hotel operator can also charge hefty fees and splits, with no occupancy guarantees.

Multi-Family Apartments

Multi-family properties typically offer better economies of scale and per unit value than single-family properties, although they are also more scarce than single family, typically cost more, and require more management.

This sector is really about five-plus–unit apartment properties. They can be small, low-rise, standalone apartment buildings, or whole complexes with many high-rise buildings.

Commercial Properties

Commercial real estate can include everything from vacant land with low management and holding costs to prime office and retail with national credit-quality tenants. Ease of regulation and foreclosure in defaults compared to residential owner-occupied homes is one reason investors choose this sector.

This sector may offer more opportunistic plays than other property types. Jumping on trends and developing areas with value-added plays can be beneficial if you know what you are doing and have the connections and experience.

Office

Office buildings have become the dinosaurs of our age. They have become redundant and unnecessary.

They can still be profitable investments, though. Many large companies run by older executives like the power and haven't been able to update themselves, or they have invested far too much in their office space to lose them or let them go.

Far more money may be made by acquiring and flipping or repurposing these buildings in the future. They can be converted to housing, industrial, and other uses.

Health

Healthcare needs aren't going away, but the real estate required in this space will continue to evolve.

Hospitals seem to continue to be very much needed. However, the typical doctor's office is certainly being changed by telehealth. So are pharmacies, with at-home delivery.

Then there are varying levels of senior care. Assisted living facilities took a big hit during the COVID pandemic. There has to be a big change there. One emerging trend is smaller residential settings for senior living. These look more like small apartment buildings, three- to four-unit residential properties, or three- to five-bedroom single-family homes.

Retail

Retail has also become a more complex sector. The real need for it has waned, although many people still prefer or enjoy getting out to the mall and shopping in person. This may be more about entertainment than the dynamics of actually needing to go to a store.

If online shopping and home delivery get better in price, convenience, and reliability, we are likely to see retail buildings as we've known them be less profitable and less essential.

Again, there are ways to augment their use and profitability, as well as repurpose them for more in demand needs.

Hospitality

Hotels, restaurants, recreational venues, and conference centers can all fall under this umbrella. Some are clearly more relevant and in demand today than yesterday.

While business travel and gatherings may be far less common for the moment, people still want to gather to eat out. They crave travel. Vices like drinking seem to do well in both great and poor economic times.

Rural & Agricultural Properties

Farmland and other acreage has its pros and cons. It can be more complex for some investors and simpler for others. It may be harder to finance and understand if you are coming from the city, but it seems that these properties may only increase in importance in the future, whether that is for food supplies, building materials, or preserving the environment.

You may find these properties becoming more popular for energy and communications, as well as for the cannabis industry. Raw land can also be used for wind farms and solar farms, as well as for cell towers.

Industrial

Industrial property seems to be picking up where office and retail have become redundant. This sector can include manufacturing, as well as logistics and warehouse spaces, R&D, and showrooms. We can be relatively certain that we'll only need more space for distribution centers in the future.

Don't forget data centers. The more and more we rely on technology, the more we need computers, servers, and places to collect data.

Mixed-Use Properties

These properties combine several functions and uses. Some malls may include office, residential, retail, and hospitality space under one roof. Townhouse projects can incorporate retail on the ground floor with floors of office and residential space above.

We may see more of these properties being developed as combined retail, office, and hospitality space. However, this also brings more complexity and challenges in financing them, selling and leasing them, and taxes.

OTHER TYPES OF DIVERSIFICATION

Geographic Diversification

There is great wisdom in geographic diversification. The three main purposes or benefits of this are:

1. Protection from the impact of disasters and regulation
2. Optimizing for rotations in market cycles
3. Consistency in performance and cash flow

All real estate is local. Your local market, the national market, and international markets are typically rotating at different phases of the cycle.

Many would-be investors won't find good deals in their local market in some periods, but going overseas often brings more complexity and risk than makes sense for the average investor. However, spreading your investments nationally can make a huge difference in minimizing risk, maximizing the upside, and enjoying consistent results.

For example, Miami and New York typically enjoy furious bull runs before crashing hard. Much of the rest of the country may follow that, but with far more muted changes. Other areas will boom as the leaders decline, although those urban coastal cities are also typically the first to rebound.

Good diversification also means keeping up the value of your portfolio at all times, and your net worth in case you need to access it.

Volume Diversification

More units are better than one. Quality is important, but don't put all your eggs into one basket. Not even a $40M house in the Hamptons.

Tenant Mix Diversification

Most of the strategies we have talked about so far (with the exception of mortgages) are focused on broad diversification. Tenant mix offers deep diversification, which is very important, as is borrower diversification. It is one of the ways many real estate investors should be graduating to the next level of intelligent investing.

Whether it is mortgage borrowers, single-family properties you are flipping, commercial buildings, or apartment buildings, this still applies. For ease of explaining this concept, let's look at examples of multi-family tenants and then strip mall tenants.

Having a good mix of tenants or users is a powerful way to achieve deep diversification. Think about a multi-family apartment building.

A really bad example of how to do this would be to rent all the individual units of an entire apartment building to a very small demographic of people, such as all employees of the same company. Then that company gets sued or broken up or everyone gets furloughed for a year due to a viral pandemic. Guess what happens? All your renters have had their incomes cut off. You get no rent. Zero. If any other jobs are out there, you might have your whole building of 400 units applying to single job openings. It's going to be rough for a while. Meanwhile, not only do you not have income or positive returns, but you still have to cover all the bills, utilities, maintenance, taxes, insurance, and more for the building. That's not going to be a fun time.

Before we get into this, it is important to be very careful about not breaching any local regulations about differentiating among and discriminating against or qualifying tenants on criteria that may be illegal in a given local market. We also have to be wary of discrimination in general, or anything that may be construed as discrimination, even if that is not our intent.

Income Diversification

It is clearly wise to have more employment and source of rent diversification in your portfolio, and even in individual buildings.

You don't want to risk everyone running out of rent money at the same time. Instead of all tenants working at the same company, it would be far better to have a diverse tenant base who gain their income and rent money from different sources.

There are three main buckets here:

1. Government-paid rent
2. Earned income
3. Retirement income

Government-paid rent proved invaluable in the COVID lockdowns. While some landlords struggled with eviction moratoriums, stay-at-home orders, and business closures, the government kept on paying the rent for Section 8 tenants like clockwork.

Other similar local government rent programs may exist, depending on where you live and hold real estate assets.

When it comes to renters who work for a living, it is wise to have them from a spread of industries. You do not want everyone working at the same employer. You don't even want everyone working in the same industry, whether it's tech startups, investment banking, local retail, or restaurants. Break it up as much as you can. This way, when one industry or sector is struggling, the other tenants are probably seeing an increase in pay and hours of work.

Some tenants may be living on retirement income. How strong and consistent they will be may depend on the source of that retirement income. If they have all their retirement income in publicly traded stocks, you could find that they are all broke next quarter when dividends are slashed and values crash.

Length of Tenancy

Leases and other renting strategies can be used for deeper diversification.

Amateur investors and landlords typically default to the traditional annual lease, which runs from whenever a new tenant shows up.

However, if you plan a conversion, major rehab, or demolition and rebuild, you may want to structure all leases to end at the same time, even if you end up with a mix of annual, 10-month, and six-month leases in the first year.

Staggering leases is another way to be in position to take advantage of local market spurts in demand when more competition exists among prospective tenants, and they are willing to pay more, such as the summer up north, or winter down south. This alone could make a 50% to 100% difference in your rental rates. It ensures you can frequently bring people up to higher market rents, while avoiding taking on lower-rate tenants during any soft periods.

Mixing up short-term and long-term tenants can be smart, too. You never want your building or portfolio to empty out all at one time, unless you need it to.

Mixing up lease lengths can help smooth out income and returns, as well as elevate returns with premium rents and avoid the risks of things like eviction moratoriums.

For example, using Airbnb-style short-term rentals, seasonal rentals, and extended-stay leases, which provide high rents and low eviction risks and costs, along with traditional annual leases and multi-year long-term tenants, which mean less wear and tear, unit turns, and management.

Price Range Diversification

A price and market segment mix provides even deeper diversification.

Each level of the market turns at different phases of the larger real estate market and economy. Each has its own advantages.

This may call for including everything in your portfolio from affordable housing or commercial property in C class neighborhoods to prime luxury units. The high end of the market may offer larger amounts of cash, while the lower end may offer higher percentage returns and more resilience in recessions than the middle market.

It is now also more common to find a mix of units in the same condo or apartment building, or new development. This may include government-subsidized affordable units in the same building as more expensive ones.

Maintaining this diversification in neighborhoods, communities, and cities has long-term sustainability benefits, too. It may help moderate taxes. It can ensure that despite some gentrification, local and essential workers can still afford to live there. That will make a big difference in the inflation of essentials like groceries and eating out, as well as the quality of teaching at schools and in emergency services. It may even make all the difference in access to labor and labor costs for your own projects.

The strip mall is another example of this that can be applied to many mixed-use commercial properties.

Yes, large "anchor" tenants and chains that are considered national-credit tenants can be attractive. They appear to be strong financial risks and often take on long-term leases and attract other tenants and traffic to your assets. Of course, in turn, they are going to be the most demanding and want the lowest rent deals. And just because they are a big international company doesn't mean they won't go bankrupt and leave you hanging. It happens all the time.

Other smaller tenants, such as independent local businesses and startups, may not have the same credit rating, financial strength, or track record. Yet they are probably less demanding, and willing to pay much higher rental rates, with lease terms that are more favorable to you.

Again, it is wise to have a mix of tenants that will even out performance in all economic cycles and through major industry changes. Discount stores will do well in recessions, while luxury retail does well in bull runs. Essentials like grocery, fast food, auto shops, and even vices (smoke and head shops, liquor stores) may continue to perform well at all times. Cars don't stop breaking down in a recession. People will always have to eat. Even in the most dire financial depressions, people still find money for alcohol — often even more of it. (Not that I am promoting these types of businesses or behavior in any way. This is just an example of diversification based on facts and data.)

You can probably see how all this also applies to borrowers and mortgage debt investing, only they are paying mortgage payments instead of rents.

Not only is broad diversification important, but baking in this deep diversification is what differentiates the performance, resilience, and longevity of the intelligent investor.

Chapter 7

KNOW YOUR ENDGAME BEFORE YOU START

Chess Grandmaster Jose Raul Capablanca, who held the world title for seven years, said, "In order to improve your game, you must study the endgame before everything else. For whereas the endings can be studied and mastered by themselves, the middle game and opening must be studied in relation to the endgame."

Sun Tzu, who is considered one of the greatest strategists of all times and whose wisdom has spawned many bestselling books over the past 2,500 years, said, "Every battle is won or lost before it is ever fought."

Stephen Covey, author of *The 7 Habits of Highly Effective People*, listed "Begin with the end in mind" as the second-most important habit. (Number one is to be proactive.)

Let's just say that if the world's best and most respected minds think knowing your endgame first is so important, we probably should, too.

You're not going to get the results and outcomes you want unless you have clarity about the endgame and results you want. You won't get them by just following the other sheep and dumping money in a 401k; money market account; or the fund of funds of public stocks that chain investment advisor told you to put all your money in, just like their last customers. Nor will you win by just chasing the next exciting investment promise with the supposed biggest returns.

That would be like taking off across the country from West Palm Beach and hoping you make it to Seattle with no map and no GPS. You can imagine how well that would go, right?

If you just want to go on an adventure and risk getting lost, without care for whether you'll end up penniless and attempting to hitchhike and beg for food in a few months, that could be a fun way to set out.

It's just not going to work if you need money or have real goals.

My friend's wife runs some Airbnbs. He says that every single month, you can count on at least one guest to get lost on their way. Instead of following the GPS link provided to every guest, some guests think they can wing it their own way. They inevitably get lost.

You can't help someone who chooses to ignore directions. Keep in mind that you could get shot for pulling up at the wrong property, and cellphone service or accessing your GPS will be nearly impossible once you do get lost. Still, people just keep on doing it.

The point here is that you have to be very clear about what you want out of your money and in terms of your money and life later. You have to be clear about that *right now*, or you aren't going to get the results you seek.

Only then can you put the pin on the map, or plan and get the directions you need to get there.

Some key questions intelligent investors ask in this process include:

- How much money do I need to retire?
- How much do I want to leave for my family or causes I care about?
- How much passive income do I need to count on to replace my earned income today?
- How much of a nest egg or net worth do I want to build?

You can go further out, and identify what that money should deliver in terms of lifestyle, opportunity, security, and freedom. Money is the tool to get there, and since we're talking about investing, we are using that as a proxy for these other outcomes.

Another extremely important principle that no one can afford to miss is that each decision and investment must be taking you closer to those goals. Otherwise, it is taking you away from it.

Once you have your goals and targets, that is your decision-making guide for everything. Every penny you invest.

This might look something like:

1. I will have a net worth of $5M within 10 years.
2. I will have $100,000 in passive income per year.
3. I will have strong downside protection so I can never risk my portfolio value being down more than 50% at any one moment.

The good news is you still have time to adjust, get it right starting today, and make the best of the mess or progress you have created so far.

Know your endgame and the outcome you want, and invest focused on that.

PORTFOLIO ALLOCATION

Diversification and portfolio allocation go hand in hand. Getting the mix right can depend on a number of factors. These can include:

- Age
- How much you have to invest
- Your timeline
- Stage of investing (growth versus preservation)
- Personal risk tolerance
- Asset classes you believe in
- Personal investment goals
- Market cycles
- The typical mix of investments often includes:
- Cash
- Cash-like low-yielding accounts and assets
- Stock
- Precious metals
- Alternatives

Alternatives are a growing and expanding asset class. Today, this includes outliers like crypto and NFTs, as well as luxury assets (or liabilities) like cars, art, and wine.

Real estate is considered an alternative because it doesn't fall under the classifications of public stocks, bonds, or cash.

Alternatives are making up an increasing part of portfolio allocation, with real estate and related investments making up the biggest portion of this bucket, so you may now have 30% to 70% of your investments in alternatives, with the 70% in real estate-related investments.

These can include:

- Direct investments in real estate
- Real estate-backed debt
- Private equity and private real estate funds

Chapter 8

THE PROS & CONS OF TYPICAL FUNDS

For many reasons, the most experienced and savvy investors are increasingly choosing funds as their preferred way to invest and diversify.

However, not just any fund will do. In fact, most are seriously counterproductive, so let's look at why to invest in funds, what makes the vast majority of funds pretty horrible, and what to look for in a good one.

THE CONS OF TYPICAL FUND INVESTMENTS

What makes most fund investments so bad for your finances?

Here are some of the reasons that they may not be serving you well, or nearly as well as you think, as well as some of the criteria you should be investigating before picking one.

Performance Records & Metrics

One of the biggest gotchas with most funds is their performance metrics. The averages they use are almost always manipulated to show far stronger results than the average investor can expect. They are arranged to skip and leave out, or at least to smooth out, the deep, deep losses most of their clients will actually experience. They may have some great runs, too. But if your portfolio is only worth 30% of what you invested when you want to cash it out, or its performance is only a third as good during the five years you are in it, that's a big problem.

Know how they are calculating these claims, and look deeper and all around to see what they aren't telling you, as well as what those other figures may mean about what you are likely to experience yourself.

Low Yields

Most funds are not high-yield investments. Some may edge into the double digits in some great years, mostly in bull run periods when everyone is enjoying far higher yields and it is hard to lose money.

Watch your net. If the fund is only targeting a 4% return, then minus fees and taxes, and factoring in inflation, you are probably losing money and taking on far too much risk to be in a losing investment.

Poor Diversification

Some funds may not be diversified enough. A more common concern is probably that they are too diversified, especially when you get into funds of funds. Or funds of funds of funds. You might end up with 1,000 or more varied stocks in different industries. The few strong performers aren't going to make enough difference to outweigh the mediocre and poor performers.

Opaqueness & Lack of Transparency

There may be little clarity about what you are actually investing in, or it is made to sound so complex that you don't want to try to understand it. You need to know what you are investing in. At a minimum, you want to understand the thinking of your money managers and what is driving their decisions. With the best managers, the individual assets aren't so important. If you can trust them and their strategy, it's best to let them do their thing.

No Control or Value-Add Potential

One of the obvious downsides of funds, and especially publicly traded stocks, is that you have no control over the value of your assets. It doesn't matter how much you shop at Apple; you aren't going to lift your stock price. Not even if you buy 1,000 of the latest iPhones.

Contrast that with homes or apartment buildings that you can renovate or raise the rents on, or commercial buildings where you can add extra leasable square footage.

No Downside Protection

Funds based on publicly traded stocks offer no downside protection. Even multi-billion-dollar companies go bankrupt, often leaving little in the way of assets to be liquidated to pay investors or benefits owed to employees. We all know someone who has seen their stock portfolio dive by tens of thousands of dollars overnight. With no downside protection, you can go to zero and have nothing to reinvest or build back from. You need real, tangible assets as collateral to protect your capital.

Layers of Funds

Onions have layers, and it may have been cute to say Shrek had layers. But layers of funds in your portfolio may give you more ogre-like results than you'd like.

There may be feeder funds and family offices that invest in funds with great results. However, when you are in funds of funds of funds, it gets pretty messy. This is not always done purely for risk diversification, but also to try to work on those various financial goals simultaneously, such as income, preservation, and growth — but it can become so fragmented that you aren't really watching, so diluted the results are too watered down, and so expensive in layers of fees that you aren't making much progress. You can end up with more of the stink than you'd like and crying from these onions in your portfolio.

That's a big difference in being able to make progress on these goals simultaneously in one fund.

Too Big

Bigger isn't always better. In this space, size does matter. You have to have a fund that is big enough to have the capital, financial strength, and track record to gain access to the best deals and pools of assets. Up to a certain point, your spreads get a lot better.

However, some investment firms and funds have become so bloated that the benefits have peaked and begun to decline.

They become limited when they must invest in hundreds of millions and billions. It's too inefficient and costly for them to make smaller investments. This means fewer opportunities for investing. Yet they have to choose between deploying that capital at all costs, even in assets that are 50% overpriced, or sitting on the money for years and having to cover payouts to their investors without bringing anything in.

Supersized organizations often end up with so many employees and layers of decision-making that they are very slow moving, and their overhead is so large and heavy that it eats up most of the potential gains.

Fees, Fees, Fees

Make sure you know what you are really paying in fees. One of Tony Robbins's most recent books focused a lot on just how dangerous fees are. They will eat your portfolio alive if you are not careful. Are you paying upfront setup or account-opening fees? Ongoing management fees? Performance-based fees? Minimum fees? Transaction fees? Exit fees? All of them?

Of course, you want your money managers to be well compensated, because you want them to be experts and to do a great job. You want their interests to be aligned with yours, though, and for you to make a fair net profit.

Overtrading

Overtrading is considered a common issue with old-school funds. Too much trading within a fund is often used simply to generate transaction fees and commissions, without concern for the financial damage it costs investor clients.

Unreliable Dividends

Dividend stocks can be beneficial. Unfortunately, most brokers don't guarantee them — there is no guarantee those dividends and income will be the same next quarter or next year. If they aren't, then you'll have to pay to switch to something else. Fear of scaring investors leads companies to make self-sabotaging short-term decisions to artificially prop up these metrics.

Interest Alignment

Most legacy funds do not share alignment with their investor customers. When regulations have been threatened to force them to act in their customers' best interests, they have often declared that they will close investment and retirement accounts because it just doesn't make sense for them anymore. That should be a huge red flag.

Typically, the advisor, broker, or manager has zero money of their own in the investments they make for you. They only make money from trades and commissions on selling to you, not from investing their own money in what they are recommending. Then they take their commissions and put them in real estate, private lending, and other types of funds.

I feel that there is enough money for everyone in good investments. You shouldn't promote something you wouldn't put your own money in, and that isn't healthy enough for your own personal portfolio. On the other hand, when you do find something great that you have proven and are getting great results from, it seems selfish not to share that information with others, and even opportunities to participate in the results you are getting when you can.

When your advisor or manager is investing in the same thing, at the same level, and their success is directly tied to yours, there is a big difference. They are heavily motivated to help you succeed and profit.

So, with all of this in mind, why invest in a fund?

THE PROS OF GOOD FUND INVESTMENTS

Good funds do pack in a lot of advantages. Here are some to look for.

Tax Savings

Especially when it comes to real estate, many tax-savings benefits can exist. This may depend on exactly how you are investing, although they may include tax-saving exchanges with long-term compounding benefits, investing through tax-deferring vehicles, or even those that provide tax-free gains. Others may include tax loss harvesting, depreciation, accelerated depreciation, and tax breaks for making certain investments in certain places.

Speed of Investing & ROI on Your Time

Investing in a fund is pretty fast. It's a lot faster than waiting 30 days to close on a home, or maybe 90 or more on a commercial property, even after you've searched, vetted, and found a deal. Not to mention all the other time that goes into direct investing.

Spending a few minutes versus hours over a period of weeks and months to make an investment makes a big difference, especially when you consider a fund can instantly put you into many assets versus all that work for just one.

Our time is the most scarce and valuable thing we have. We each only have so much of it. It is imperative that we constantly demand the best ROI on our time that is possible.

Exposure to Liability

Direct investment in real estate can be a major liability. It's sad but true. There are ways to minimize that liability with legal entities to hold titles in and layers of insurance. If you can invest without any of that personal liability, it is just smart to do so.

All it takes is one professional criminal to steal your title or make up a lawsuit, and it can cost you everything. You may still lose everything, even if you win the legal case after years of fighting it.

When you invest through a fund, you don't have any of that liability. That is passed on to the fund, and to those it employs to handle transactions and management. The fund can also have its own insurance and can finance a far stronger legal team than individual investors can handle alone. Often, just having those layers of protection and a feared legal team is plenty of deterrent to send the criminals and opportunists back to looking for individual and unprotected investors to victimize.

Remember: Intelligent investing is about risk-adjusted returns. This is a method for shaving and insulating against a lot of risk. Whether it is accidental, frivolous, malicious, or criminal, owning, managing, marketing, and selling real estate can be a virtual minefield of liability.

But it's still worth it.

Better Access

Unless you are personally in the top 1% of the top 1%, you just can't get access to the volume, quality, and discounts on deals that a fund can. It may not seem fair, but that's the way it is. A fund can get you that access and pay for itself in the process.

Beating Personal Capital Limitations

No matter how much you have to invest you are limited. The same goes for how much you can borrow personally. Even if you have several million to invest, that won't go too far in real estate by yourself. Even if you can get more than 10 multi-million-dollar mortgages yourself, not everyone wants to personally guarantee that level of debt and repayment.

A fund enables you to invest along with other accredited and intelligent investors — not only spreading your risk, but being able to take advantage of more opportunities than you could or would alone.

Consolidated Organization

It's often the little things that get you. Juggling a lot of properties or note assets alone, or even with a small less-experienced team, brings some risks you may not expect.

One of the hidden gotchas is missing paperwork, mail, and email notifications. These can be notices alerting you to potential title fraud, changes in ownership, or mortgages being put on one of your properties. In the past, issues have occurred with miscellaneous property tax-related fees and force-placed insurance.

If you miss these notifications, you could lose your asset or equity, or at least end up in foreclosure, even if you didn't make a mistake in paying the bills.

This gets increasingly complicated as you grow a wisely diversified portfolio. It is a full-time job. It can be a full-time job for a whole team of people.

With a good fund, you don't have to worry about that. It is all monitored for you, with clean, regular, or real-time reporting.

Professional Management

Professional management is critical. If you've invested in any rental properties before, used an agent to buy and sell, or run a rehab project in the past, you have probably already had a taste of this.

The importance and complexity rise and are compounded as you begin diversifying in more asset classes and more assets. Especially in different jurisdictions.

With a fund, you get all this baked in — professional management and its value for limiting liability and enhancing performance.

True ROI vs. DIY

As intelligent investors gain experience, they eventually come to the same realization: Doing it yourself doesn't always lead to the best possible ROI.

You can only do so much diversification yourself or with a tiny team. That will always limit your results, and keep you exposed to more risk. It's real work, too.

When you dig into the math, after taxes and including your time and all expenses, the truth is you probably aren't making any more than the best fund will return you. Yet you are doing all the work and taking all the risk on yourself.

Real estate can be a lot of fun. There's no reason you can't run a renovation project or commission the building of a property you've always dreamed of on your own. Just distinguish this fun and hobby work from actual investing.

Do the math yourself, weigh the benefits, and see for yourself.

Simplicity

For many of the reasons above, good funds offer an incredible amount of simplicity.

You should never trade simplicity for taking on unnecessary risks, exposure to loss, or negative yields, but when you can gain more, with more safety and simplicity, it's just smart.

This simplicity means freedom and peace of mind, not stress and running around like a chicken with its head cut off. There's little point in having all the wealth in the world if you are miserable all the time.

Chapter 9

FUTURE-PROOFING YOUR FINANCES WITH A HYBRID FUND

What it comes down to is that we all want to invest for great returns, while being confident in our financial futures, right?

This realization led me to a hybrid fund.

All my experiences in business, real estate, finance, intelligent diversifying, and navigating the constantly cycling market and unknowns have brought me to a hybrid fund as the answer.

It is a concept that seems to be gaining steam since this concept and new asset class were first pioneered a few years ago.

How does it work? What's inside it? Is it right for your investing efforts?

WHAT DOES "FUTURE-PROOFING" MEAN?

Future-proofing can have several applications. It boils down to insulating your finances and investments from future events and protecting the desired outcomes.

Recession-proofing or recession-resilient assets and investing are one part of this. Of course, a recession isn't always looming, and you don't want to limit your upside unnecessarily.

A true hybrid fund will certainly include recession-resilient assets and investments that see enhanced performance during recessions and economic depressions, although it goes beyond that as well.

Structured correctly, your portfolio should also insulate you against disasters and other unprecedented events — some may say "the unexpected." Yet, when you have time to think about it, few things are really unexpected or not foreseen. Their timing may certainly come as a surprise, but even tornadoes, tsunamis, asset bubbles, economic collapses, changing regulations and trends, and global pandemics are all anticipated. It's just a matter of where, when, and how great their impact will be.

These are all factors accounted for in a strong hybrid fund.

It is a collection of investments, strategies, and correct structuring that minimizes these impacts, while empowering your upside; again, bringing together wealth preservation, passive income, and wealth growth. All with the ease and simplicity of a great fund investment.

It is about creating a portfolio and managing it so your money, returns, and what it is supposed to deliver for your life is there when you need to count on it.

Something that most investments promoted over the past few decades have performed horribly at doing.

WHAT IS A HYBRID FUND?

A hybrid fund brings together the principles of intelligent diversification in multiple assets, combining multiple asset classes, and developing investment strategies. In this case, we are specifically talking about a fund that brings these strategies and diversity together under one umbrella: real estate.

What's in a Hybrid Fund?

Depending on the market, timing of your investment, and other factors, a hybrid fund may include:

- Single-family homes
- Multi-family properties
- Commercial properties
- Tax liens
- Performing mortgage notes
- Nonperforming mortgage loan notes

Strategies that may be deployed in a hybrid fund include:

- Value-add investing (fix and flip, repositioning, etc.)
- Opportunistic investments
- Buy-and-hold income-producing investments with various leasing methods
- Loan workouts
- Note-flipping

Flip back to previous chapters to revisit the purposes and advantages of these individual asset types and strategies as a part of your portfolio.

KEY ADVANTAGES OF A HYBRID FUND

Among the reasons to invest in a hybrid fund are:

- Simultaneously achieving multiple objectives
- Future-proofing your finances
- Solid tangible assets
- Above-average returns
- Passive income yields
- Consistency and predictability
- Simplicity

HOW CAN YOU PARTICIPATE IN A HYBRID FUND?

There are a variety of ways to begin reaping the rewards of a hybrid fund and see the difference it can make in your investing success and finances.

These are some of the most obvious.

Invest Directly with Cash

As an accredited investor, you can invest directly into a hybrid fund with savings, earnings, and other investment funds.

Minimums, preferred returns, length, and target returns may vary depending on when and which fund you choose to participate in.

Invest through Your Retirement Accounts

Although the tax treatment of these accounts may change over time, self-directed IRAs, 401ks, and similar vehicles can offer tax-deferred and even tax-free gains. Trusts and other entities may also participate.

These may all offer additional tax advantages, as well as ease of succession and inheritance planning.

Invest through Your Own Fund

Clearly a lot in organization, recruiting, structuring, legal filings, and more goes into establishing a hybrid fund and building a track record of success in such funds.

However, if you are an existing fund manager, then you can invest funds on your clients' behalf into a hybrid fund, with someone who has done all the hard work and has the structure and the track record.

This is a great way to deliver premium results to your clients, attract more of them, and benefit from financial arbitrage, all with the simplicity of a fund investment. You can focus on your expertise and put your time into gaining investors and serving them well instead of spreading yourself too thin on all sides. It can reduce your workload by half and amp up your results.

Others who are already accomplished investors may seize this opportunity to graduate to creating funds of their own. You can create feeder funds with the purpose of investing that capital into a hybrid fund, and again benefit from that arbitrage.

GETTING STARTED WITH HYBRID FUNDS

If you are already quite happy with your investments and current returns, but want to see what you are missing out on and ensure you and your clients are future-proofed, it is worth testing the waters with a hybrid fund.

Check out the current minimums in great hybrid funds that check all the boxes, and put some capital to work as a test. Experience the difference and rebalance your portfolio accordingly as it works out for you.

As you are doing your searches, be sure to check out the results of NNG's hybrid funds and how we are doing it over there. I'm sure you will find inspiration and food for thought.

Conclusion

Thank you for reading.

You may have opened this book already understanding how valuable and critical real estate is to your finances and future. You may already have been trying to practice the timeless principle of diversification.

No matter whether you are just getting started and are trying to get an early edge, or you are an accomplished investor or veteran fund manager, I hope you have found some great nuggets, some reminders, or fresh insights to think about.

As you can see, there is a lot more to diversification than most understand. It's common sense to upgrade your diversification, deeper and broader. Not only in assets, but in strategies as well.

For many reading this, a fund may emerge as the answer to building more confidence in their financial planning; future-proofing their money and lives; and intelligently optimizing the upside, with attractive risk-adjusted returns, too.

You may choose to begin diversifying on your own, or even create your own fund to participate in the benefits of the hybrid model.

Whichever path you embark on, and wherever you end up finding your conviction about the best way to balance your investing, I wish you the best, and hope you are able to share these vital principles with many others.

Whatever you do, just get started . . .

About the Author

Investor, wealth manager, educator, and proud father of two incredibly financially savvy sons, Fuquan Bilal has spent more than 21 years operating businesses and perfecting his proprietary formulas for investing in real estate and other alternative asset classes.

When he's not in the office, you might catch Fuquan running to the gym, experimenting with new tweaks to his personal performance, taking on new challenges, exploring new markets with his kids, or hosting the Passion for Real Estate Investment (PFREI) podcast.

As the founder and chief visionary officer of NNG Capital Fund, Fuquan has proven to deliver to investors through a variety of funds over the years, most notably when it comes to providing attractive risk-adjusted returns and achieving predictable levels of passive income.

He is one of the few leaders in this arena who has proven to come through and level up through periods of national and global economic distress and prosperity.

What may really separate Fuquan from others, in addition to his magnetic personality, is the care he has for sustainably managing his clients' funds, as well as managing his teams and treating them well, and caring about the communities where his firms operate.

While these may seem fluffy to some, they are absolutely the differentiator when it comes to survival and the ability to thrive for companies, funds, and reputations, and all of those counting on them.

If you haven't yet, be sure to catch up on Fuquan's first two books (available on Amazon): *Turning Distress into Success*, about how to navigate tough markets, and *The Tire Kicker*, about taking action.

www.ingramcontent.com/pod-product-compliance
Lightning Source LLC
Chambersburg PA
CBHW071715210326
41597CB00017B/2487